Winning the Spiritual War

by Dr. James Holland, Sr.

Copyright © 2009 by Dr. James Holland, Sr.

Winning the Spiritual War
by Dr. James Holland, Sr.

Printed in the United States of America

ISBN 978-1-60791-137-1

All rights reserved solely by the author. The author guarantees all contents are original and do not infringe upon the legal rights of any other person or work. No part of this book may be reproduced in any form without the permission of the author. The views expressed in this book are not necessarily those of the publisher.

Unless otherwise indicated, Bible quotations are taken from The Spirit Filled Life Bible NKJV. Copyright © 1991 by Thomas Nelson.

www.xulonpress.com

TABLE OF CONTENTS

Chapter 1 Choosing Sides 7
Chapter 2 The Battle for Authority 13
Chapter 3 The Boot Camp Of Obedience 23
Chapter 4 Why Should I Be a Soldier "Servant?" 31
Chapter 5 Get Ready To War! 39
Chapter 6 Understanding Your Enemy 51
Chapter 7 Our Secret Weapons 61
Chapter 8 Taking Back Lost Ground 73
Chapter 9 Behind Enemy Lines 79

CHOOSING SIDES

Every human on the planet must choose which side he or she is going to be representing as they walk through the minefield of emotions, events, anger, dreams, disappointments, joy, and sadness that make up what we call life.

Make no mistake about it; we are all on one side or the other. The spiritual battle lines have been drawn. If we are going to win this spiritual war, then the first order of business is to decide which side we are on; the side of light or the side of darkness.

In the pages that are ahead, you will find spiritual laws that, when applied properly, will supersede the laws of nature and guarantee our victory in Christ.

When I was growing up, we had a lot of neighborhood softball games as well as basketball games.

Regardless of what the game was we played, the first order of business was to choose sides. No game can be engaged in until the teams have been chosen. Then to play the game properly you had to have a reasonable understanding of the rules of the game and know the objective of the game.

I still remember on some of those hot summer afternoons as we engaged in the softball game that some of the older kids had a tendency to make up rules as the game moved forward, especially if it was in their favor, or else they would slightly bend the rules.

Of course, as time went on and some of us younger guys became the older guys, we did the same thing. Any new kids in the neighborhood that would question our rule bending or rule making would be quickly reprimanded and informed that, "that's just the way we do it around here." We were the players, the rule makers, the umpires, and the determining factors of how the game would end. Unfortunately I was of the mindset that this was the way it was all over the world! That is until I became old enough to, shall we say, visit other neighborhoods and witness real games being played at neighborhood ball fields and, where I might also add, they had real umpires and real coaches.

Unfortunately, it seems that many Christians endeavor to live the Christian life this way as well, just making up rules as they go along. Of course, their response is normally the same as ours was when challenged, "it's just the way we do it here!" This is the cause of much defeat, confusion and immaturity in many Christians. My friend, this game we are in must be played by the rules of combat and then we will be victorious. Victory is not some elusive butterfly that we are constantly reaching for. Satan wants you to think that victory is just ahead or either just behind you.

The scripture, however, is very clear on the subject of victory. It's not ahead or behind us, it's something we walk in and live in! Victory is our daily walk! It's our position in Christ!

So then, the question on the floor is, "Whose side are you on? If you have been born again, then you are on the Lord's side. However, there are rules of engagement that you must not only know, but put into practice. You must identify with these rules to be a winner. God doesn't honor emotions, good intentions, or good ideas. He honors the Word. His Word is the rule book. I might add, we have no authority to change or bend the rules. If you are confused about whose side you are on, then you are a prime target for Satan.

If we are on God's side then we must stop living like we are on the devil's side. Don't allow Satan to intimidate you. Know the rules of the game. We have been given the battle plan and all the weapons we need to win this war!

IDENTITY CRISIS

You must remember everyday that you walk onto this battlefield of planet earth, who you are. This is no time nor is this the place to forget whose side you are on and who you are in Christ.

WE ARE CHILDREN OF GOD!

I Peter 1:23 declares that we are born of imperishable seed. That equates to the fact that royal blood is flowing through our spiritual veins. John writes in I John 3:1, "How great is the love the Father has lavished on us, that we should be called children of God!"

WE ARE HEIRS OF GOD!

Before we were born again, we were slaves to sin and Satan. Yet, Galatians 4:7 declares we are no longer slaves but sons of God and also heirs. Being an heir means we are going to inherit something of value. Paul reminds us of this inheritance in Romans 8:17. He says we are co-heirs with Christ, which means we have everything He has purchased and made available. **EVERYTHING!!**

My friend, when we are on God's side then we are on the winning side. It is, however, imperative that we understand this. We must identify with the body of Christ.

WE ARE SEATED WITH CHRIST!

Ephesians 2:6 Says, "And God raised us up with Christ and seated us with Him in the heavenly realms in Christ Jesus."

What does this really mean? To be seated with Christ is, first of all, a position of honor. Sin disgraced us, but salvation exalted us to a place of honor in God's kingdom! This also means that our position in Christ is one of being given the authority to live by and through the authority that is in the Name of Jesus Christ! It is impossible for us to win this spiritual conflict unless we understand and operate in our rightful authority and dominion over the works of our enemy.

JUSTIFIED IN THE SIGHT OF GOD!

What exactly does the word justification mean? Does it imply that I can do anything I want to do and God will come along and clean up my mess? That God will make excuses for my actions? The answer to these questions, of course, is NO. The word justification means to be made just or righteous. Romans 5:1 says, "Therefore, since we have been justified through faith, we have peace with God through our Lord Jesus Christ." God has made us just. That is, our guilt has been replaced with forgiveness. Our shame has been excused and joy has come in its place. God has made us a part of His family through the new birth. This is something to shout about!

A NEW CREATION

2 Corinthians 5:17 says, "Therefore, if anyone is in Christ, he is a new creation, Old things have passed away behold all things are made new!"

To be on God's team means I do not have to live in the fear that somehow God will not give me complete victory in my life. As strange as this may sound, there are millions of believers who actually live under the deception that they can only be victorious in certain areas of their lives. Nothing could be further from God's truth.

This kind of thinking is like a pregnant lady saying, "I am about half pregnant!" Of course, this is impossible, either the lady is pregnant or she's not. There is no such thing as a half pregnant woman!

My friend, from God's perception, there is no such thing as a half victorious Christian. God has in fact declared that we will win this war. So, if you are truly born again, you are not some patched-up, wired together person. You have been given a new heart, a new mind, a new life and you are in a new family. GLORY!! As new creations, the guilt of our sin is gone, and God's express image is restored in us. We have become a new and an especially designed work of God. 2 Corinthians 3:18 declares, "We are being transformed into His likeness with ever increasing glory."

ALL WE NEED
2 Peter 1:3 says, "According as his divine power hath given unto us all things that pertain unto life and godliness, through the knowledge of him that hath called us to glory and virtue." Read this verse slowly so that it may soak into your mind and your spirit. He hath given us (past tense); it's not coming, we've already been given everything we need! His power in us continues to sustain us and keep us from falling. We must, however draw down from the heavenly throne these resources so that they may flow in our daily lives.

WE ARE VICTORIOUS!
Paul writes in Romans 8:37, "In all these things we are more than conquerors through him who loved us."

What does "all things" mean? It means anything that life or Satan will ever bring against us. With God we can overcome it! Notice also the word "more", not just conquerors. That would be great, but we are more than conquerors. We not only can win this war, but we can also enjoy our victory now.

SPIRIT FILLED!
Part of the new birth is the infilling of the spirit of God into our lives. We see this pattern all through the new testament. In Acts 1:8

Jesus declares "ye shall receive power after that the Holy Ghost has come upon you and ye shall be my witness." In Acts, chapter 2, we see this promise fulfilled and thus the new testament church was birthed.

Being a believer is Christ living in us not merely around us. Paul used the phrase *"In Christ"* 44 times in his writing to the church. We must be in Christ. That's what the new birth is all about. Don't settle for just being around Christ. Don't settle for just going to church. You can know about Christ and yet not be in Him! You can go to church and yet not be in the church. "In Christ" is what we must be for the power and weapons of the heavenly kingdom to be released and made available unto us. Many Christians are defeated by Satan simply because they forget who they are in Christ and also because they forget whose side they are really on! Shout it every day that you get up "I am a child of God!" I am on the Lord's side!"

More scriptures on being spirit filled:

ACTS 19:6; ACTS 8:6-8; 12-20 ISAIAH 28:11; 12 ACTS 10:44-46 MARK 16:17; ACTS 11:15 ACTS 2:1-4; I COR 14:18 ACTS 2:33; I COR 14:21-22 JOHN 3:1-8; ACTS 1:4-8 ROMANS 8:23-27; ROMANS 14:17 TITUS 3:5; I JOHN 3:24

PRAYER:

God remind me of who I am in Christ. Help me to remember daily that I am forgiven, I am born again, and I am spirit filled. That I can and will walk in victory today. That no weapon formed against me shall prosper. That you are with me and that I will win this war for my soul. In Jesus Name. Amen

THE BATTLE FOR AUTHORITY

People don't like the idea of authority. The word *authority* is an ugly word for many in today's society. Yet, in order to live with victory over the world, the flesh and the devil, we must submit to the authority that God has set over us. Resisting authority comes naturally to us because of Adam and Eve's rebellion against God. Unfortunately, not only is the idea of submitting to authority not popular in the world, neither is it popular in the church.

Yet, we must ask ourselves the question, "What is the end result of a generation (both in the church and out of the church) that has cut its teeth on anti-authority ideas? Jesus prophesied that the last days would be mocked by a spirit of lawlessness (Matthew 24:1-12). In Luke 9:1, Jesus gave the disciples power and authority over the satanic powers of wickedness. In this scripture the Greek word for "power" is **"dunamis"** which means ability and strength, the Greek word for "authority" is **"exousia"** which means the official right. The truth we must realize is that the freedom and authority we have in Jesus Christ is because we are under his authority. The Christian life does have its stern, unyielding requirements. <u>**There must be a law if there is to be liberty.**</u>

Psalms 119:54 says, **"Thy statues have been my songs in the house of my pilgrimage."** The Law of God is a song in our life. The train, as powerful as it is, must have a track to run on. The mighty seas, as magnificent as they are and as powerful as the waves and currents may be, are yet hemmed in by the shore line. The stars, the universe, the sun, and the moon are all held in their position by the pull of gravity. If there is to be liberty then there must be a law as well! Jesus said, **"Ye shall know the truth and the truth shall make you free!"**

In this hour, we as Christians, must understand spiritual authority. Christians are not just people that look good and conduct themselves in a nice and acceptable way. We are children of the king and He has given His authority to us to win this conflict for the souls of men. The life God desires for us is one of authority. Once we understand this and begin to walk in it, we will see the glory of God in our lives daily. This power and authority is for us today, right now, not just somewhere in the sweet by and by.

Satan will gather all the forces of hell and the demons of darkness to keep us in ignorance about God's authority that can be released in our lives. Satan wants us to think that victory is impossibility. Read Romans 8:35-37 **"Who shall separate us from the love of Christ? Shall tribulation, or distress, or persecution, or famine, or nakedness, or peril or sword? As it is written, For thy sake we are killed all the day long, we are counted as sheep for the slaughter. Nay in all these things we are more than conquerors through him that loved us."**

The key word in this passage is *through*. Through what? Through Jesus Christ. His power, His authority, and His glory as it is being released in our lives as we walk in His authority by submitting our will to His. The believer should walk on conquered ground each and every day. Before sin cursed the natural world man had authority over all created things. Adam's dominion was over the beast of the field, the fowls of the air, and the fish in the sea (Genesis 1:28). Yet, when God drove Adam and Eve from the garden, that authority was lost.

It is important at this time to point out that living the spirit-filled life does not exempt us from the consequences of the physical curses that are still in this natural world. We have been given spiritual authority over the world, the flesh, and the devil. *World*, in this sense, means the sinful lifestyle and mindsets that its society promotes. Make no mistake about it, God has given his people spiritual authority over the powers of our enemy. We must be careful not to become sympathetic with the enemy. This is a trick of Satan that he uses on many. How does it work? People that become sympathetic with the enemy begin to think and say things like, "as long as I am sincere, that's all that matters "or" I know what the Word says, but," or, here's another one, "well, I am justified in my wrong thinking or action because of what has happened to me."

Satan doesn't get alarmed simply because we go to church or pray from time to time! He doesn't get too alarmed even when we are born again because he knows that many born again people will continue to act and think just like they always have. They will also continue to respond to life and disappointment just like they always have. Why? Because they do not understand how to walk and live in the spiritual authority God has made available to them.

ENEMIES OF AUTHORITY

God gives spiritual authority to his children who have a spirit of submission. **How we behave under pressure is a sure sign of what is really going on with us!**

A classic example of staying submissive to authority is David in the Old Testament. Saul, the then reigning king over Israel, had authority over David. Yet, Saul was insane with jealousy and had forsaken the running of the kingdom to devote all of his time to hunting down David to kill him. While David used wisdom in running for his life, he still kept a submissive spirit. David understood authority even when it was being abused.

While hiding in the cave at Engedi, Saul actually came into the cave where David and his men were hiding. Now, the men with David believed this to be God delivering Saul into the hands of David so they said, "God hath delivered him into your hands." Notice what David said to Abishai, "Destroy him not for who can stretch forth his hand against the Lord's anointed and be guiltless?" (1 Samuel 26:9).

This is why understanding spiritual authority is so vital to our victory. Even when those who are in authority over us are not doing properly, if we will stay committed to the chain of command that has been set in place, God, in His time, will honor our submission and bring a great victory. It wasn't long after this encounter that David assumed the throne to be king.

When Nathan, the prophet came to David while he was king and exposed his sins with Bathsheba, notice what David did. He didn't challenge the prophet and say, "Who do you think you are; I am the King." No David repented and pleaded for forgiveness. Again when Nathan came to the aged king and said "You will not build this temple but your son will". David didn't rebel against the word of the prophet, but rather he submitted to it. There is a price for submission.

I Peter 2:19-20 declares, **"it is good to endure grief and wrongful suffering with patience for the sake of God."** Yet, without submission there will be no spiritual authority in our lives. The results of a non-submissive spirit is the spirit of rebellion.

MANIFESTATIONS OF REBELLION
The most obvious areas of our lives that rebellion to God's authority will show up are in our *words*, our *reasons*, and our *thoughts*.

Ephesians 5:6 tells us to **"Let no man deceive you with empty words: For because of these things cometh the wrath of God upon the sons of disobedience."**

Matthew 12:34 declares **"for out of the abundance of the heart the mouth speaketh."**

Our words are the outlet of the heart. A man who is rebellious in his heart will soon utter rebellious words. Look at what happened to Eve. She carelessly added to God's Word. When she was tempted; she added "neither shall ye touch it" to God's word (Genesis 3:3). This was a serious mistake on Eve's part.

Anyone who really knows and understands the authority of God's Word would never add to it or take away from it. God's Word said, **"of every tree of the garden thou mayest freely eat: but of the tree of the knowledge of good and evil, thou shalt not eat of it."** (Genesis 2:16-17) God never said **"touch not"** this was added by Eve.

All who easily change God's Word, either by adding or by deleting gives evidence that they do not know authority. Look at Ham and what he did when he saw his father's nakedness. He went out to tell it to his brothers. Ham jumped at the opportunity to reveal his father's fault. All who are insubordinate in heart will always expect the authority to fall. In fact, they rejoice in it! Ham outwardly submitted to his father, but it was only half-hearted. We can not walk in this spiritual authority and still have rebellion in our hearts for those in authority that God has placed over us. There are two things which will cause Christians to lose their power; sin and reviling of authority.

REASONS

Our rebellion against authority is manifested in word, in reason, and in thought. When we do not submit and honor authority, we will speak slanderous words. These areas can become strongholds of our making for the enemy to enter in and fight against us.

Ham, in his mind, had reason to slander his father because Noah was naked. Miriam spoke against Moses on the basis of the fact of his marriage to a Cushite woman. If we are subject to authority however, we will live under and by that authority and not by mere reason.

Korah and a company of two hundred fifty leaders spoke out against or actually rose up against Moses and Aaron. Their reason was God is with us just as he is with the both of you. So why should we look up to and follow you. The answer, of course, was because these men were the authoritative leadership that God had ordained. If we are going to follow the Lord then we must be delivered from our reason when it would cause us to rebel against the authority that God has placed in our lives. What army can be successful if the troops refuse to follow the chain of command of authority that is in place? The answer is that no army will be successful with this kind of reason, neither will the holy army of God's people.

Let's talk about ourselves. Where do we live today? When God's command comes to us, do we stop and consider the matter to see if there is sufficient reason for us to do what God has spoken? This is a manifestation of the tree of knowledge of good and evil. The fruit of that tree governs not only our personal affairs. Even God's appointed things have to pass through our reason and judgment **We think for God and decide what God should think!** This is why it is so easy for us to talk ourselves out of what God is instructing us to do.

We must either live by God's authority or live by human reason, it is absolutely impossible to live by both. The earthly life of Jesus proved this. What reason could there be for the disgrace, the lashing, and the crucifixion which he suffered? Yet, he submitted Himself to God's authority. He neither argued nor questioned. He only obeyed. He knew His purpose for being here. Jesus said consider the birds of the air and the lilies of the field. How simply they live. The more we are subject to authority the simpler our lives will be.

GOD NEVER ARGUES!

Have you ever found yourself arguing with what you knew God would have you to do? Come on now, be truthful. We need to remember we are not called to be God's counselors. He is God and He has the authority to do what He likes. We can't follow Him on the one hand and on the other hand demand to know the reason. We must stand on the ground of obedience to His word.

GOD'S PRESENCE

It is not easy to be delivered from slanderous words. It is even harder to be delivered from reasoning. We must live in God's presence where He is manifested. We will discuss this manifestation of God's power in depth later, but for now, know that we can't survive spiritually outside of the presence of God in our lives. Only those who live in darkness can live by reasoning. Since the time when Adam sinned by taking the fruit of the tree of the knowledge of good and evil, reason has become the life principle of man. It's only after we have been in the presence of God and His glory has appeared to us do we realize that we are but dead dogs and lumps of clay. All arguments fade away in the light of His glory.

I read somewhere some time back these eye-opening truths about man. "A man weighing 176 pounds lives in a body that contains enough fat to make nine bars of soap, enough iron to make one nail, enough phosphorous to make a few hundred match heads, enough water to fill a nine gallon can, and enough sulfur to de-flea one SMALL dog. In all, he is worth about $23.79 on the open market." Inflation factors not considered. Yet, we are going to argue with God? Go figure!!

REBELLION THROUGH THOUGHTS

2 Corinthians 10:4-6 (Darby Translation) **"For the arms of our warfare are not fleshly, but powerful according to God to the overthrow of strongholds, overthrowing reasoning's and every high thing that lifts itself up against the knowledge of God and**

leading captive every thought into the obedience of the Christ, and having in readiness to avenge all disobedience when your obedience shall have been fulfilled."

Rebellious words come from rebellious reasoning, and reasoning has its birth in the thought process. 2 Corinthians 10:4-6 is one of the most important passages in the Bible when it comes to winning this spiritual war. Let's look closely at verse 5, **"leading captive every thought into obedience of the Christ."**

Paul declares we must destroy every high thing that lifts itself up against the authority of God in our lives. We love to build reasons as strongholds around our thoughts. Paul says these reasons must be dismantled and our thoughts brought back under the authority of God's word in our life. In spiritual warfare the strongholds must be stormed before the "thought" can be taken captive. Paul is instructing us not to use reason to fight against reason.

The mental inclination to reason must be met with spiritual weapons, the name of Jesus, the Word of God, and, of course, the spirit of God. Our mental habit of reasoning is something we inherited from the tree of the knowledge of good and evil, yet many of us never realize how much difficulty these minds of ours give God! Satan certainly takes advantage of our carnal reasoning. If all of our reasoning is carnal, then of course, our thoughts will be carnal. When carnal reasoning rises up, our thoughts fall into a trap of carnal thinking.

CAPTURE THAT THOUGHT

In the Greek New Testament the word **"noema"** or **"noemata"** in the plural is used six times. Philippians 4:7; 2 Corinthians 2:11, 3:14, 4:4, 10:5, and 11:3.

The English translation of this word is *"thought"* or *"thoughts"*, which means the device or devices of the mind. **"Mind"** is the faculty; **"Device"** is its action, which is the product of the human mind. Through the faculty of the mind we freely think and decide what we will be and do. Our actions represent what and who we are. To release God's authority into our lives, we must overthrow our carnal reasoning. This will not happen until we see God as our God and the seat of authority in our lives. This is why many Christians don't behave very well sometimes. They may say I know what God says about this, but! They are held in captivity by their carnal reasoning and carnal reasoning produces carnal thoughts!

They are not under spiritual authority. They are under their own fleshly authority. Satan loves this! It is only when our thoughts have been captured and brought into agreement with the words of Christ that His authority can rule in our lives. This is what the mind of Christ is all about. It's not about some fuzzy feeling. God's authority, once released in our lives will overthrow all the strongholds that Satan has erected in these areas of words, reasons, and thoughts. This is walking in the authority of the spirit.

Consider these scriptures to release in your spirit:

ECCLESIASTES 8:4; NUMBERS 23:8 EZEKIEL 25:5; ISAIAH 22:22 ROMANS 13:1; MATTHEW 16:19 COLOSSIANS 2:10; MATTHEW 18:18 I CORINTHIANS 4:20; ROMANS 9:21 Ecclesiastes 8:4; "where the word of a king is, there is power."

PRAYER:

God give me understanding that I may bring my words, my reasoning, and my thoughts under submission to your Word which is your authority that you desire to release in my life. I give you permission to work in my life that I may live under the authority of your Word, your name and your spirit. I repent of being lead by my carnal reasoning and my carnal thoughts. I realize these things war against what you are trying to do in my life. I submit and I surrender to you today. Make me a winner in this spiritual war I am engaged in. In Jesus' name I call this done! Amen!

THE BOOTCAMP OF OBEDIENCE

"All that the Lord speaketh, that must I do."
Numbers 23:26

"Neither God nor Satan can use a disobedient servant."

If you survived the last chapter on the "Battle for Authority in our Lives," then you are a candidate for the "Boot Camp of Obedience."

Obedience can be compared to the autobahn in Germany. On the autobahn you can travel as fast as you desire. There are no red lights, no stop signs, and no traffic jams.

Most of the Christian world, unfortunately is traveling on the expressway of "do it my way," "it seems right to me," or this one is really jammed, "God will understand". There is a blessing in obedience that can only be experienced by being obedient.

Submission is a matter of attitude, while obedience is a matter of conduct. **Matthew 7:24; "Therefore whosoever heareth these sayings of mine, and doeth them, I will liken him unto a wise man, which built his house upon a rock."**

Often in our society today, the word *obedience* strikes at the heart and makes us uncomfortable. We resist the Lordship of Jesus Christ. Our carnal nature wants to have its own way with complete control of our lives. Of course, this is not good.

When we are in control we give in to the cravings of the flesh and soon find ourselves in trouble with God. It would appear from the scripture that obedience is absolutely necessary if we are to have the authority of God's Word released in our lives.

THE TEST OF SURRENDER

If you have ever gone to a real military boot camp you know it's about as far from a church picnic as one could get. Yet, it is there that military forces are built! Many of them will defend us and this great land so we definitely want them to be acting in obedience to those who are over them. Obedience is all about surrender. Surrender is the next step after commitment.

Step 1: Commitment.

It goes without saying, if we are not willing to make a commitment, we will not go far in God's great army. What is commitment? It is agreeing to do something. We commit to prayer; we commit to give; and, we commit to each other; yet, we are still in control! Many Christians need to empty themselves of themselves so they can be filled with God! While it is true that commitment is the first step, we must go further if we are going to really be obedient!

Step 2: Surrender.

To surrender means I will do as I am instructed! In Titus 1:1 Paul says he is a **"doulos"** of Jesus Christ. This word refers to a slave. It speaks of one who is in a permanent relationship of servitude to one whose will is swallowed up in the will of another. In the New Testament this word is often translated to the word "servant." We can't win the war of obedience until we surrender to the power of God that is released in our lives. Then and only then will it be easy to obey.

When the spirit of rebellion leaves us, then will the spirit of obedience be quickly restored to us and the church. Who then are we to surrender? The Lord Jesus Christ!! Lordship is the secret to a surrendered life. To be Lord over someone or something depicts total absolute power and authority. Jesus is referred to as Lord no less than 747 times in the New Testament. Sometimes, we think we are going to make him Lord. You can't make Him Lord, He is already Lord. **The question is, is He Lord over our lives?** Do we live a surrendered life to Christ? Then and only then can we and will we walk in obedience. There is strength to obey through our surrender. Do you want the power of the Name of Jesus released in your life? Do you want the anointing of the spirit flowing on a regular basis? Then here is the secret to it all. We will never be over those things that God has set under us until we learn through obedience to be under those things that God has placed over us!

Jesus declared that no man could serve two masters. They couldn't in the days while Jesus walked upon the earth, and my friend, they can't today either. Jesus is not the least bit interested in a "part time kingship." He must be Lord and King in our lives at all times.

Jesus will settle for no less than absolute ownership of all we are. This means unquestioned obedience. In Luke 6:46, Jesus asked, "Why call ye me Lord, Lord, and do not the things which I say?" If we are going to win this spiritual war, then we must be Christians walking in obedience every day of our lives. That includes our work place, our witnessing, our friendship, our families, and all that we engage in. Many in the Christian community are afraid of this level of obedience. In fact, they call it fraternization. May I tell you we certainly need "more trees that produces more lumber and fewer nuts in the kingdom." However, this is the level of true obedience that the apostles and the early believers walked in and may I remind you that we are still inspired by their lives in the kingdom. Hell could not delay them, nor handle them. The power of God's authority flowed through them and entire cities and regions were delivered from sin and Satan's grip.

OBEDIENCE VERSES SACRIFICE

In I Samuel 12:14-16, the prophet Samuel is charging the people of Israel to be obedient to the commandments of God even though they now had a king over them. Look at what he is saying in verse 14, **"If you fear the Lord and serve Him and obey His voice, and do not rebel against the commandments of the Lord, then both you and the King who reigns over you will continue following the Lord your God."** Not much room there for doing things our way! Verse 15; **"However, if you do not obey the voice of the Lord, but rebel against the commandments of the Lord, then the hand of the Lord will be against you, as it was against your fathers."** When we do not walk in obedience, the hand of the Lord is against us. This is not good!

Because many do not understand how God views obedience, there is almost uncontrolled rebellion within the ranks of God's army. No, they are not robbing banks. In most cases, they are not committing hideous acts of sin. Yet, they are living for God on their terms! So there is either none or very limited authority of the spirit in their lives.

King Saul had this problem as well. We read in I Samuel 15:19, **"Why then did you not obey the voice of the Lord?"** Samuel the prophet has confronted the King. Look at Saul's response in verse 20 when he said to Samuel, **"But I have obeyed the voice of the Lord and gone on the mission on whom the Lord sent me."** What Saul is actually saying to the prophet is "I did it my way." Of course this is not obedience. Verse 22, **"Then Samuel said, "Hath the Lord as**

great delight in burnt offerings and sacrifices, as in obeying the voice of the Lord? Behold, to obey is better than sacrifice, and to hearken than the fat of rams."

Here is God's perspective on disobedience. Verse 23, **"For rebellion is as the sin of witchcraft, and stubbornness is an iniquity and idolatry, because you have rejected the Word of the Lord, He also has rejected you from being King."** Saul's whole train of thought was that I'll just do it my way and God will accept it. Saul was never interested in obeying what God said; he merely wanted to just get by. Saul's answer to everything was to just give God a sacrifice, to just try and temporarily satisfy God's demand. My friend, we can make all kinds of sacrifices, yet if we are not living in obedience to God's Word we still will not have the blessing or the approval of God. Millions go to church services every week and are under the deceptive mindset of believing if they just give an offering or something of that nature, God will excuse their total disobedience to His word, nothing could be further from the truth!

IT GETS WORSE!

In 1 Samuel 15:34-35, we read some very disturbing words. Verse 34; **"Then Samuel went to Ramah, and Saul went up to his house at Gilgal of Saul.** Verse 35; **"And Samuel went no more to see Saul until the day of his death. Nevertheless, Samuel mourned for Saul and the Lord regretted that He had made Saul King over Israel."**

This is always the end result of disobedience. Saul lost his prophetic voice in His life. As we engage in the Kingdom of God in this final conflict, we must not overlook the fact that God demands *obedience* on our part. It's not enough just to go to church. It's not enough just to be in God's army. It's not enough just to have a general understanding of what God's Word says. We must be walking in obedience to the word if we are going to win this war. I remind you, it is God's will that we win. If we don't, it won't be God to blame! Allow the spirit of God to search you right now! Let His spirit do a search and rescue mission in your soul now. We must not lose the prophetic voice of anointing; we must not lose the power of the spirit that is released in the obedient life! Saul's life continued to have a downward turn. He finally ended up at the home of a witch. My friend, God has placed you and me in the greatest kingdom in the universe. Yet, all that God has made available to us will avail very little in our lives without obedience!

THE BLESSINGS OF OBEDIENCE

Just as there is a curse of disobedience, so there is a blessing that goes with obedience. We must realize this early on! Do you want to get out of boot camp? Do you want to have the promises of God's Word released in your life? The secret to all of this happening is our obedience to God. Remember until you and I surrender to God, we will not walk in obedience. God instructed Joshua to lead the Israelites to march around the city of Jericho for seven days and then shout its walls down. Just image how that command was received by the people. I am sure there were some objections and alternative suggestions, yet, God said do it this way. The victory was secured in the act of obedience! I am sure with Joshua's military experience he had another plan in mind. Yet, he turned a deaf ear to carnal reason and obeyed God's command. He put aside his own plans and obeyed his Lord. Can we do that?

Obeying God's commands is also our secret to victory over sin and Satan. In Luke 6:47 Jesus says, **"Everyone who comes to me and hears my words and acts upon them, I will show you whom he is like."**

Notice the three characteristics of this person. First: He is deep in his trust. Jesus said that he is like a man building a house that digs deep and laid a foundation upon the rock (verse 48).

When you walk in obedience you are not soon shaken. Your trust in the Lord is not superficial. Your spiritual roots will go deep. What is the evidence of all of this? **OBEDIENCE!**

The second thing about the obedient hearer of the Word is that he is durable through trials. Jesus says, **"When the floods came, the house could not be shaken."** The floods symbolize times of overwhelming grief, or loss, or tribulations and personal afflictions. Even the obedient warrior can expect the hour of crisis to flood his life. Jesus is saying that when you obey Him you will survive every storm that may come your way.

We must walk in obedience even when we don't understand what is going on.

Third: The obedient warrior is defended against his temptations. Jesus says, "The house could not be shaken because it had been well built (verse 48). The river bursting against the house is an illustration not only of trials but also of temptations that threatens our spiritual lives. The well-built defense against these satanic assaults is a **faith that obeys**.

Everyone is building some sort of life. It should be one God can bless. In the parable, both the obedient man and the disobedient man built a house. One suffered great loss, the other one was victorious! The difference was obedience! Stop saying you are no match for Satan. God would not send us to war if He had not intended for us to win. We are more than a match for Satan's attacks when we are walking in obedience. This is the secret to victory. In contrast, Jesus describes the disobedient man. Look at what the Lord says:

First of all, he is detached from the Lord. He represents all those who always want to take a short cut to winning the war. All those who attend church, listen to a sermon, hear the Bible being taught, even read the Bible, and say they believe it all, yet they do nothing about it. They have Christian beliefs, but not Christian behavior. They gain outward respectability as religious people, yet they do not dig deep and do not invest time in the inner room of prayer. They do not yield themselves to the indwelling power of the spirit of the Lord.

The second thing about this listener is that he is defenseless without the Lord. Jesus said of this man's house that when the flood waters came, the house collapsed immediately. It had no stability at all. If our faith is only on the surface, evidenced by our lack of obedience, we will be blown away by life's difficulties.

Finally, this can be said about the person who listens to the Lord, calls Him Lord, but does not obey Him. He is deceived about the Lord. James cautions us in James 1:22, **"But prove yourselves doers of the word and not merely hearers who delude themselves." (NAS)**

What do mere hearers of the Lord delude themselves about? Their relationship to Him!! **Neither God nor Satan can use a**

disobedient servant! If we obey God, then our obedience becomes a key to open the promises of God to us. God has many tremendous promises for those who are serious and willing to obey Him.

PRAYER:

God, I repent of any disobedience in my life. Please cleanse me of my rebellion of wanting to do your will my way. Give me the strength to walk in obedience to your word. I understand that it is your will for me to be victorious! Deliver me now that I may obey you In Jesus Name. Amen

WHY SHOULD I BE A SOLDIER "SERVANT?"

"Serve the Lord thy God with all thy heart and
with all they soul."
Deuteronomy 10:12

It is difficult to comprehend biblical servant-hood in such a self-serving world as ours! There are those who would say the secret to greatness is connections, influence, and perhaps financial clout. Yet, God's view is very different. God says the secret to a great life is learning how to serve.

> **Matthew 20:26 says, "Whosoever wants to become great must be a servant of others." God says the way up is down. The more you serve, the greater you are. Jesus said, "For even I didn't come to be served but to serve others and to give my life as a ransom for many." Jesus made it very clear that he came to serve. You and I are in the kingdom to serve the purpose of God. We were created for service. Also in Ephesians 2:10 the writer says, "For we are God's workmanship, created in Jesus Christ to do good works."**

God has allowed us to be alive that we might serve his purpose in this world! We are not born again just to be born again. We are born again for His service. We are waging war against the spiritual forces of evil that want to destroy God's plan for our lives. Yet, we must recognize that God has gifted us for His service.

As believers we are commanded to serve. Did you get that? Read it again, slowly. We are commanded to serve. It's not optional, it's not just for when I am having a great day. It's not just when serving is going to make me look good. A sign of maturity is that I am interested in serving. Immaturity is evidenced when all I am concerned about is "who is going to meet my needs?"

> **Romans 7:4 says, "You are part of this body of Christ and you belong to Him..."**

Service is evidence that Christ is in us. If you are a believer, you are part of the body of Christ. If you are not active in service then the whole body will suffer. This is why Satan loves to see God's people get on this "it's my ministry and my program kick."

HELPING OTHERS

How do I serve God? **Colossians 2:3 says, "Whatever you do in word or deed do all in the name of the Lord."**

I serve God by not only being involved in the church and making my talents and abilities available, but I also serve God when I help someone else.

When is the last time you took someone to the store that had no way to get there? Or, cut someone's grass that was not able to do so, or prepared a meal for someone who was not able?

This is service. We owe God everything, yet we don't serve God out of duty, nor do we serve Him out of fear or guilt. We serve God out of love, gratitude, and joy. Being a true servant of God makes life meaningful.

Some give their life away for a career and get a gold watch at the end of 35 years. Some give their life away for recognition, and some for pleasure. The truth is, everybody gives their life away for something. The question then, is am I going to give my life away for the right thing? It is not just how long one can live that matters, but how you live that really counts.

We need to remember we all will give an accounting of the life, talents, and abilities we have and what we do with them. Spiritually speaking, we don't need to just get the basics and no more. We need to get all God has available for us so that we may be truly victorious.

POWER THROUGH SERVICE

The most potent power in the world is <u>**servant power**</u>. It can never be misused because it always obeys God. It will always accomplish what it's intended to because God will back it all the way. It will do only good because the Lord God of Glory is its source, sustainer, guide, and goal. The true leader is a servant. Servant power begins to be released in our lives as we make a commitment to serve. Too many Christians are running here, there, and everywhere. At some point in your life, you have to stop running, stand, and fight! As we are talking about servant power, let's consider an example from the Bible. Job received his miracle of healing and restoration when he prayed for his neighbors! **That's SERVICE!**

Jesus said give and it shall be given. This is not restricted to offerings and tithes. We give of our lives. When the widow gave her limited substance to the prophet, there was always more in the barrel every time she returned to it. Service is giving out so that we may receive in. We must understand this in the hour in which we live. What effect could we have on this planet if we would really become servant soldiers of Jesus Christ? This late hour demands no less. The power of the spirit of God is released when I involve myself in His service. Because of this, we must be sensitive to the needs of others. We must serve and we must give our wills to be placed in His hands for molding. Our talents are given to speak for Him, and our lives are given to reproduce His own life within us.

When we serve in a servant leader capacity, God will reveal His will to us. We must always ask ourselves," how is my dedication to others?" Are we dependable even in crisis? Are we dependable to God, to our friends and to the church?

REAL SERVANTS HAVE HUMILITY

When the disciples had gathered with Jesus for His last meal, they were somewhat shocked at what He did. He washed their feet! He also let them know unless you are willing to serve others at the lowest level, you can't really be a part of *His* Kingdom. How willing are we to stoop down to do some things that we may even think are beneath us? Can you work behind the scene or must you always be in the spotlight? Do you take on the task that no one else will do or just the ones that bring the high praise? Are we really willing to put ourselves aside and serve the Lord with gladness? God has created us to be servants. If you want to be a servant (and you should because it's our calling) then you are in the right place at the right time.

There are three ways to miss the right time. You can arrive early. You can arrive late. Or, not arrive at all! There is something in the spiritual realm that seems to be saying to us that today is the right time. God needs servants, not advisors!

THE MIND OF THE SERVANT!

How should the mindset of the servant focus on this world and the task before us?

I Corinthians 2:16 says, "For who has known or understood the mind (the counsels and purposes) of the Lord so as to guide and instruct Him and give Him knowledge? But we have the mind of Christ and do hold the thoughts (feelings and purposes) of His heart."

This scripture is telling us that we, as true Servants, will see the world and people as Christ sees them. We will know our purpose and we will understand what it is God is endeavoring to do through us. We will realize it's all about Him and not about us.

According to a recent survey, there will be fifty million more people on planet earth at the end of this year than there were at the beginning of this year. WOW!! We have a tremendous harvest field before us, yet if we don't have the "mind" of a servant we will, for the most part, never see it!

In Philippians 2:5-7, we read in verse 5, **"Let this mind be in you, which was also in Christ Jesus."** Paul is telling us when we recognize our purpose as did Jesus, the spirit of God will so eclipse our flesh as it did His, that all the entire world can see is God working, instead of seeing our flesh. This is servant hood. The world has already seen too much flesh trying to fulfill the work of God! The mind of Christ is the manifestation of the spirit of God working in us. Many times the longer we live for God, the more our (flesh) increases and the less manifestations of God's spirit we have at work in our lives. This, of course, is totally in reverse of what should be happening. When this occurs we become less tolerant of others and of other things. We start telling people what we think instead of letting the spirit work in us.

The mind of Christ is allowing the spirit of God to flow through us. Listen friend, our flesh will not impress anyone nor will it deliver anyone! The more mature we become in Christ, the more the world will see God in us instead of seeing us!

Look at verse 6, "who being in the form of God thought it not robbery to be equal with God. Verse 7, "But made himself no reputation, and took upon Him the form of a servant, and was made in the likeness of men."

Notice the phrase **"made himself no reputation."** That is, He never exalted his flesh. He allowed the spirit to have such predominance that His flesh was overshadowed by the spirit. In the scripture there is very little information about the man Christ Jesus. Think for a minute. Can you tell me what His favorite color of robe was? What kind of sandals did He prefer? What kind of food did He like best? Where was His favorite eating place? Sounds strange doesn't it? Yet, He did all these things. If we want to talk about Jesus the Savior, we know He walked on Water; He healed the sick. The demonic world was subject to Him. He had power to forgive sin. He fed the multitudes, He died on a cross, and He rose again from the grave!! Hallelujah!! So we know a lot about the God (man) Jesus. As servants of God, we must be careful not to endeavor to make a reputation for ourselves! It is not necessary that the world know much about your flesh, and my flesh, but they must know about the God in us!

Question! What does Satan see most of when he attacks us? Our flesh, or our God! The mind of Christ will help us keep focused on our purpose. Remember, we will either be **"purpose driven"** or **"self driven."** This is how we win this war. The spirit of God in us is the only adequate judge for our flesh. We get in trouble when we try to judge others or ourselves. We must learn to allow the spirit in us to judge our flesh. Know that regardless of how long you may have been serving God, **that, if given the opportunity, our flesh will compromise our walk with God!** We must not only be born again, **we must live born again if we are going to win this war.** This part of servanthood has to do with behavior. Christ's behavior always brought glory to God. It also always revealed the purpose for which Christ had come to earth. So should our behavior. James says, **"give no place for the devil"** that is, don't allow areas of our lives to become strongholds of self desires that are contrary to God's purpose for our lives.

LET'S TALK ABOUT PURPOSE!

If we don't have the mind of Christ, it goes without saying, we will never fulfill the purpose of Christ in our lives. We will wonder around in our spiritual experience wondering what God is trying to do.

Look at Romans 8:28. It reads, "And we know that all things work together for good to them who love God (servants) to them who are called according to His purpose."

It is time to get the war plan right. This is not our battle, its God's battle. It's not our victory it's His. It's not about my agenda; it's about His. So, if I am going to win, I have to be a part of the called (God's army).

What am I called to do? Do things the way I want to? NO! I am called to be a servant of the most High God.

Religion is man's attempt to reach God. Yet, salvation is God's invitation to reach man. Selfishness means I am called to prove something to someone. It means I am called to convince folks to do everything my way. Selfishness also means I have to impress somebody, to promote myself, and to protect myself! Is that what Jesus did? NO!! He said, "I am come to fulfill the will of Him who hath sent me. I speak only what the Father tells me to speak."

Why are so many losing the war that we are supposed to be winning? Because they are called for their purpose instead of God's purpose. We must correct this. If I am not a servant warrior, allowing the spirit to develop the mind of Christ in me, the spirit flowing through me to remind me of God's purpose for my life instead of my selfish purpose, then I have no right to believe that all things will work together for my good.

God defends the called to His purpose, not the called to MY purpose. We spend far too much time trying to accomplish our agenda and our purpose! This is cause for much defeat and confusion in the body of Christ. When winning this war for the glory of the name of Jesus is more important to me than someone trying to exalt me for trying to merely hold on. When we minister, when we sing, when we teach, when we give for His purpose rather than for our self exaltation, then and only then will we see a great breaking forth of the power of God in our lives.

Look now at verse 29, "For whom he did foreknow, he also did predestinate to be conformed to the image of his son, that he might be the first born among many brethren." Verse 31says, "What shall we say then to these things? If God be for us who can be against us?"

Herein is the purpose of God for every Believer, **"that we might be conformed to the image of His son."** Jesus came to earth looking for the cross. Are we, as His servants, looking for the victory that is ours? Paul declares if God be for us, who can be against us? He is simply saying once we understand our call and our purpose, it doesn't matter who is against us. We will prevail.

PRAYER:

Mighty God help me to understand that since I have given my life to you I am no longer my own. I belong to you, I am enlisted in your eternal Kingdom to live and fulfill your purpose for my life. That you have created me and gifted me to serve in your kingdom. Let me be a willing vessel, let me be dependable, and let me identify my place in the kingdom to war against the powers of darkness to help win the souls of men for your honor and your glory. In Jesus Name. Amen.

GET READY TO WAR!

"He that overcometh shall inherit all things"
Revelation 21:7

**God does not demand results,
He demands obedience and action!**

There is a spiritual battle raging and it is a fight to the death. The Christian walk is not a "walk in the park." Satan is not the nice guy on the corner giving away free popsicles. Even though you may be born again, you will not merely float gloriously along into heaven unabated! Neither do we have the luxury of neutrality. We must engage in the fight. A truce will never be called.

It must be victory or else. What are we fighting for? Our spiritual lives? Our families? Our cities? Our world? Our churches must become training camps for spiritual warfare instead of shrines to be worshipped. Did you know that America leads the world in domestic Crime? America has the largest population of incarcerated people in the world. America now leads the way with the highest incidents of suicide and abortion. Four out of five people in America are untouched by church. In the next twenty four hours in America, 10,799 babies will be born and 6,403 will die. There will be 6,148 marriages, yet, in the same twenty-four hour time frame, there will be 3,110 divorces. Sounds bad, doesn't it? Lest I depress you, I won't mention many of the other problems in our world. After all, we are in a "war zone" and war is always destructive.

We must understand that our enemy is real. Although he no longer has a position in heaven, he is still allowed limited power on the earth through deception and craftiness. This is why Satan loves it when people say and believe that he doesn't exist. Satan is destroying lives by his acts of deception. It's time to go to war against him.

Notice the story in **Mark 5:1-20.** Here we see the plan for Satan for all mankind. The man in the story is controlled by a great amount of demonic spirits. Satan wants to inhabit, torment, destroy, as well as damn the human soul to outer darkness. Read the story and see what Satan has done to this poor man.

The man was preoccupied with death. Look at where he lived. He dwelled among the tombs. Satan wants to kill everything good in our lives. This man wasn't in a hospital getting help; he was in a cemetery with dead folks. **"The wages of sin is death."** Satan wants everyone to live in the **"death zone."** All of your hopes and all of your dreams, Satan wants them dead. Notice also that this man could not be controlled. The spirits in him rebelled against any kind of authority. Satan wants people to believe that God doesn't want them to enjoy life or to be blessed.

Yet, Jesus said in **John 10:9-10, "I am the door, by me if any man enters in, he shall be saved, and shall go in and out and find pasture. The thief cometh to kill and to destroy. I am come that they might have life, and that they might have it more abundantly."**

Which do you want?

Notice also the demonic man in the story had neither clothes nor any sense of decency. That's how Satan works. He desires to remove all sense of decency and dignity from human life. Also in verse 5 of the story, it says; **"and always day and night he was in the mountains and the tombs crying and cutting himself with stones."** Our generation is under siege by Satan. It's time to do something about it. Our generation also seeks peace from a pill in a bottle or a needle in our veins. Yet, none comes. Notice also the self-mutilation and destructive acts this man was engaged in. Why does Satan want to make us miserable?

Because we are created in the likeness and image of God. So when people, through sin, destroy and abuse their bodies, it's just like slapping God in the face. Then, we see in this story that this man, because he was possessed, was separated from his family and friends. This is always Satan's plan, to divide us or separate us so that he may conquer us.

Question! What stones are cutting at you? At your family? Is it the stone of lust to do everything your way? Is it the stone of rebellion? "I know more than anyone else?" Is it the stone of "living for the flesh," thus abusing your body and destroying your health by pushing your body to the extremes just to please someone or yourself? Is it the stone of separation from friends and family, which normally identifies itself with words like, "I don't fit in," or "they don't understand me" or, "I do better by myself?"

Then, finally notice what effect these spirits had on this man when Jesus showed up. **"But when he saw Jesus afar off, he ran and worshipped him, and cried with a loud voice (the demonic spirits) and said, "What have I to do with thee, Jesus, thou Son**

of the most High God? I adjure thee by God, that thou torment me not" (Mark 5:6-7)

Let me point out something here. It is true that this man came and worshipped Jesus, which proves that no amount of demons can stop us from worshipping God. Yet at the same time, his worship did not bring peace to him for the demons cried out. Even though they had to come under submission to Jesus, they still did not love or respect Jesus. Neither did they want to give up total control of the territory they were in. Many today reach out to the Lord only to get relief instead of deliverance. The spirits that have ruled their lives will endeavor to possess some other area of their lives or their families even while they are worshipping the Lord.

This is why there must be deliverance, total deliverance instead of relief! If you read the rest of the story, you will see that this man did receive total deliverance. Yet there is another strange twist. The town's people seeing him clothed and in his right mind were afraid. They asked Jesus to depart from their coast. They had become so acclimated to sin and its destructive power that they felt uncomfortable when deliverance and righteousness was present. Sound familiar? Listen friend, not everyone will be excited when you and those you love are truly delivered and when our cities are experiencing true revival. But we must understand that we are not here trying to win a popularity contest; we are at war for our lives, our families, and our cities, as well as our nation.

CHOOSE LIFE

The scripture is very clear on the matter of salvation. Everyone must be born again. That is the mandate. Yet, in this war zone, once we are born again, then we must begin to live out this new life.

Most Christians only engage in spiritual warfare with a hope of either relieving present distress or attaining a somewhat normal existence. Victory begins with the name of Jesus on our lips. It is, however, consummated by the nature of Jesus being developed in our hearts.

Remember how the Lord delivered Israel out of Egypt so He could bring them into the promised land? Likewise, we are delivered out of sin, not that we might live for ourselves, but rather that we might come into His likeness and His purpose. If our life's goals do not align with God's, then we will invariably find ourselves entangled in the same problems that caused our difficulties in the first place.

RELEASE GOD'S POWER IN YOUR LIFE
In this spiritual warfare we are engaged in, we are never alone. God is with us. It's about who's for us and who's against us. Did you know that God uses a very predictable process to release His spiritual power into our lives? We must know and understand this truth. If we don't, then we will spend a lot time discouraged and wondering what's going on!

God releases His power in us through faith. The Bible declares, "without faith it's impossible to please Him." Yet millions are trying to please God in all other kinds of ways. Here is God's process.

Faith, when released, will produce a dream, an idea, a vision, if you please. You will be able to begin to see yourself victorious, being blessed of God, and doing the will of God. With God, there are no accidents, only divine appointments. Ephesians 3:20 says, **"God is able to do far more than we would ever dare to ask or even dream of – infinitely beyond our highest prayers, desires, thoughts, or hopes."** (L.B.) However, a dream is worthless until we decide to do something about it.

Probably for every ten dreamers, there is one decision maker. This is where most "wonderful" Christians stop.

When you make a decision, you are deciding to invest your time, money, energy, and reputation to live victoriously. The truth is, if you want to walk on water you still have to get out of the boat. As much flack as the Apostle Peter has taken from saints and preachers alike about him walking on water and then sinking, I remind you, to date, he is still the only disciple that has ever walked on water. He is still the only one who made the decision to get out of the boat. Condemn him if you will, but I remind you he has walked on more water than the rest of us! James 1:6 says, **"But let him ask in faith, nothing wavering. For he that wavereth is like a wave of the sea driven with the wind and tossed. Verse 7continues, "Let not that man think that he shall receive anything of the Lord." (NKJV)**

After our faith produces a dream, that dream then pushes us to a decision. We must know that there will be delays. There is always a time lapse before your vision becomes reality. God uses this waiting period to teach us to trust Him. Always remember delay is not denial. **God says, "These things I plan won't happen right away. Slowly, steadily, surely the time approaches when the vision will be fulfilled. If it seems slow, do not despair, for these things will surely come to pass. Just be patient! They will not be overdue a single day." (Hebrews 2:3) L.B.**

Then problems start showing up. The two most common types of problems are critics and circumstances.

In **1 Peter 1:6-7, the scripture says "at the present you may be temporarily harassed by all kinds of trials. This is no accident, it happens to prove your faith, which is infinitely more valuable than gold." (PH.V.)**

If we are not careful, while God is building our faith, we will become like King Hezekiah. Isaiah, the prophet, under direction from God, went to the King and delivered the message **"set your house in order, you are going to die."** Hezekiah had no problem receiving the word from the Lord. In fact, he turned his face to the wall and began to pray. What a prayer it must have been! Before Isaiah had left the grounds the word of the Lord came to him again and said, "Tell the king I have heard his prayer and I am giving him fifteen additional years to live. Isaiah, with joy delivered the message and yet the king, though joyous, no doubt about the latest word from God, still asked for a sign that this would happen.

Sometimes, when we have encountered Difficulties, it becomes easiest to believe the worst instead of believing the best! Yet, if our faith is intact, we will believe the promise of God.

Have you ever met God on a dead end street? Dead end streets are when your situation will deteriorate from difficult to impossible. It is only when we reach these points that we are ready for a miracle! Remember, only when we have exhausted all of our abilities is the stage set for a miracle.

The final stage of maturing faith is deliverance. This is what Satan is afraid of. Because once we reach this level of victory, then our faith is so mature that we are living by faith and warring by faith instead of acting off of emotion or human reason.

GO TO WAR FOR YOUR FAMILY!

One of the greatest areas of battle is the family unit. The family was a "God idea" so Satan targets the family as the first line of attack. You better believe if the king of darkness came against the first family as a point of entry into our world, then he certainly will come at our families today.

We must fight for our families. Love isn't enough! That sound strange, but it is true. I have witnessed people that actually loved each other yet their home was in total disarray as far as the relationships between the parents and the children were concerned. The demonic forces that are now relentless in their attacks on the home must be driven back. The home is the foundational structure of a society and a nation. No wonder the battle on the family is so intense! Job 22:29 says, **"Declare a thing and it shall be established."** This is easier said than done. We need to join in with Joshua to declare, "as for me and my house, we will serve the Lord."

REALITY CHECK!

We Christians need a reality check when it comes to our homes. Somehow we have come up with some rather warped ideas about how God will protect our families. Some Christians believe that they can never work on building the relationships with their family members, and, yet, by some miracle everything will just be ok. This, of course, is not true.

Many Christians are in total disarray because their families are falling apart and they don't seem to know what to do about it. This, of course, bleeds over into their spiritual lives as well. This affects our churches! O, how Satan must love this.

I declare to you, it's time to turn the tide. What can I do? The battle front is twofold. We must build a relationship and spiritual strength at the same time. Here are some steps we can take to build relationships with our mates.

Understand your life's call is not to change each other, rather to build on the strong points of each others lives while working to make the weak areas strong. Constantly work on communication skills.

There are five basic levels of communication needed for spouse and children.

Level 1: SPEAKING IN CLICHÉS "How did your day go?" "What have you been up to?" "How are you doing"

Level 2: SHARING FACTS: Talking about the weather, bills to pay, world news, repairs on the house or car.

Level 3: STATE OUR OPINIONS: "How could you do that?" "That was stupid?' "What were you thinking?" Our words are powerful and we need to choose them wisely.

Level 4: TRUE FEELINGS: At this level of communication you become transparent with each other. You let them know what you really feel, yet not in an ugly way. Many families are operating year after year at level one or level two and wonder why their family is falling apart.

Level 5: REVEALING REAL NEEDS: This is where you have heart to heart talks. You open yourself up for your spouse, parent or child to encourage each other. If we are not at least partially successful at this level, then it doesn't matter how spiritual you are trying to be, it's all out of balance. Our relationships with each other is vital for true victory. No marriage can survive on auto pilot. Many people, even in God's kingdom are in a marriage, yet they don't have a marriage!

LISTEN UP GUYS!

Treat your wife with strength and gentleness. Give her complete praise and reassurance. Define areas of responsibility. Avoid criticism. Always, always remember the importance of the "little things." Recognize her need for togetherness. Give her a sense of security. Recognize the validity of her moods. Cooperate with her to improve your marriage and your home life. Always try to identify and meet her individual needs.

YOUR TURN LADIES!

Here are just a few things that you wives can do that will help us men who sometimes don't even know that anything is wrong until it's broken down completely. Study to pay attention to your husband. Don't always be reminding him of who you wish he was really like. Regard him, that is, try to do some things with him that he enjoys doing and this, of course, should be practiced by the husband toward the wife as well. Honor him. Do not try to belittle him or embarrass him in public. Build on his strong points. Always reconfirm to him that you want him to be the spiritual leader of the house.

We must also remember as parents that we are consistently building relationships with our children. While it is true that all of our relationships will go through several different phases through life, it is important that we never stop the building program!

WHAT ABOUT THE SPIRITUAL FRONT?

We must engage in spiritual warfare by exposing the strongholds that Satan has established in our families.

In Acts 16:31, it says, "Believe on the Lord Jesus Christ, and thou shall be saved, and thy house."

Job offered sacrifices and prayer for his children and their families daily. We must do the same. The Word of God has creative and protective powers when released into a family that is in unity. We must remember the wages of sin is always death. So don't be deceived into thinking if your children or your mate isn't doing right that somehow God will understand and make adjustments in their case. This is a spirit of deception! I have witnessed parents, as well as mates, become so discouraged with family members that they just give up and begin to make statements like, "well I guess there is nothing I can do after all, I can't make them do right or serve God."

This is a manifestation of a spirit of deception that brings with it depression as well. While it is true we can't make or force anyone to serve God, we certainly can intercede for them to such a level that God will begin to drive back the spirits that are influencing their wrong actions. We can deliver such prayer power that there will be such an air attack of the spirit of God that the loved one can't enjoy their sin any longer! So pray for your mate and your children regardless of their current condition. Believe God's Word to work and give it time to work. The work of the devil and his cohorts is to destroy us. This is not the will of God! It is not God's will for our children or our families to be destroyed by sin. We were created in "His likeness and image."

Pray over your family daily; lift up a "prayer hedge" and the spirit of God will maintain that hedge for us. We must drive the forces of darkness out of our homes.

WAR FOR YOUR CITIES!

It doesn't really matter where you live, there is work to do. We must take spiritual authority over the influencing spirits that give our city its personality.

2 Corinthians 5:20 declares us to be **"Christ's ambassadors."** What is the difference in an ambassador and the average citizen? Authority. Our ambassadors that are sent to the many different countries to represent our president and our country always transact their business in the name of the President and the government of the United States of America. By the same token, we go into enemy territory "in the name of Jesus Christ, the King of Kings." **In Matthew 16:18, Jesus gave us some keys to the kingdom.** We can open the gates of Heaven as well as charge the gates of Hell until the gates fall and we go in to bring deliverance to the city. We need to focus our prayers not only on the people in our church, but on our city as well. The church is in the city to declare and to regulate spiritual authority in the area. Even in the churches that actually take time to pray for their cities, I dare say not many of them go into the streets of the city and drive or walk up and down them praying for the power of God to begin to move in these areas! The command is to go and not sit back and see what might happen! If there are particular sins that are more prevalent in our city than others, then let's target them first in prayer. Question! How do you act where you live? Do you conduct yourself like everyone else? Do you think like everyone else? Do you constantly complain to God about how things are in your city? Do you constantly question God for His purpose of letting you live there? As a Christian we are where we are to be used of God to make a difference. Stop this nonsense of saying, "If I could be somewhere else, I'd do better" or "If I was somewhere else God could really use me!" You better know that God can't use us where we are not. So, it

must be His will for this time to use us where we are. Stop wasting time! We Christians are not in our cities just to blend in. Neither are our churches there just to take up real estate. We are there, said Jesus, as light and salt. When we walk in the dominion of authority that God has made available for us, our cities can be changed, our neighborhood can have revival, and our churches can and will grow. So stop letting the fallen spirits and mindsets of your city dictate to you what kind of spiritual climate there will be. We are there as ambassadors and Christ's representatives. Take authority. Weep for your city. Pray over your place of employment and pray over your neighborhood. Become the solution instead of just melting into part of the problem! **Psalms 127:1 says, "Except the Lord build the house, they labor in vain that build it, except the Lord keep the city, the watchman waketh but in vain." PRAYER:** God help me to understand the war I am engaged in. I repent of anything that may be in my spirit that would hinder you blessing my life, blessing my family, and blessing my city. I realize many of the spirits that I am warring against are deeply entrenched. Yet, through the name of Jesus, I break their hold and I take authority over their influence. I declare my life, my home, and my city as a place and habitation for the Lord! I will not waste anymore time with wrong thinking and wrong motives. I understand I am in your will. That you have placed me here on the planet to win the war for your name sake. In Jesus' name I release this now! Amen.

UNDERSTANDING YOUR ENEMY

No general who is going to lead an army into battle will do so without understanding his enemy. You must know how your enemy will respond to certain situations. To understand your enemy and how he will respond and operate is a must in war if you intend to win. As I endeavor to familiarize us with our enemy, don't think for a moment that I agree with him. Nothing could be further from the truth. Many Christians have been told not to discuss Satan, his kingdom, his tactics, and his spiritual structures of demonic activities. For, in doing so they would glorify him. If you are fascinated by the dark side and you dwell on it all the time and do not serve God, then this could happen. Yet, if you are going to be victorious, you had better understand who your enemy is and how he operates. If we don't know who our enemy is, then we are not sure who to fight! It goes without saying, there is a spiritual invasion of demonic powers sweeping through our world today. In fact, many people invite Satan into their lives because they don't know their enemy. Jesus spent much of His earthly ministry delivering people from tormenting spirits. Jesus said to the church, **"In my name you will lay hands on the sick and they shall recover, you shall cast out devils."** (Mark 16:16) There is a real Devil! Yet, most of Christianity doesn't really believe that he exists. I remind you, it was a real devil that entered the garden and a real devil that tempted Jesus! It will be a real devil that is cast into the lake of fire! Satan is an accuser of the brethren! If we are always trying to accuse or dig up dirt on our brothers and sisters, then we are doing the devil's work! We are never acting more like Satan than when we are trying to pull others down and exalt ourselves! Satan wants people to believe they are defeated. The Bible declares Satan to be a fallen angel, yet he has legions of fallen spirits organized into his army. **John 10:10 gives the mandate of Satan, "He cometh to seal, destroy and kill."** Jesus believed Satan was real. **Matthew 12:25 says, "every kingdom divided against itself shall not stand."** This verse reveals three important facts to us. (1) Satan has a kingdom, (2) His kingdom is unified, (3) He is come to destroy you emotionally, spiritually, and physically. Are these fallen spirits real? Jesus thought so. He spent twenty five percent of his earthly ministry casting evil spirits out of ordinary people, most of which kept the Ten Commandments. Which means they were probably more moral than many professing Christ today!

SATAN'S CHARACTERISTICS

In the Bible, Satan is described as the adversary, the slanderer. He is known as the accuser of the brethren, the "angel of light," as Beelzebub as deceiver, as the great dragon, as the Prince and power of the air, as the ruler of darkness, as the tempter, as the wicked one, and as a roaring lion. Before his fall, he is known as Lucifer. He possessed great musical ability, and he was adorned with beautiful stones! He was the perfection of wisdom and purity. Yet, through pride, he failed. Satan possesses intelligence. He also has a will, and he possesses a memory. He certainly possesses pride and desire. He was in the garden of Eden and he is in the world today, your world, and my world. He empowers false prophets and he resists God's Word. He resists God's people when they pray and when they worship. He resists God's people when they fast. He blinds the carnal minds of men from the truth! He steals the word of God from the hearts of men. He is the author of sin. He releases fear, oppression, and depression. He is a destroyer. Satan is an unclean spirit! He promotes hate, jealousy, strife, and all manner of demented lifestyles. Before we talk about the different levels of his demonic organizations, let me endeavor to answer a question that is in the minds of many today.

WHY DOES EVIL EXIST?

What is evil? Where does it come from? The Bible is very clear about this and also provides a solution for the evil that is wide spread and entrenched in the world today. The Bible declares that evil is rebellion against God and God's plan for man. Evil is self-absorbed and uncaring of others. Evil takes and never gives. Yet, some argue that it's God's fault! They argue that since God created everything and evil exists, then God must be the author of evil? The Bible, however, paints a picture in which God, in the beginning, created perfect surroundings for Adam and Eve to live in. **(Genesis 1:31).** So, how did evil get into the picture? The Genesis account tells us that a cunning "serpent" introduced evil into God's perfect creation.

Yet, Genesis 3:1 seems to say that God created the serpent too. So, doesn't that prove, as some argue, that it's God's fault evil exists today? They argue that there may be some forces equal to or greater than God, that is beyond God's control, or maybe, just maybe, God isn't good after all?

THE REAL ANSWER

A close study of the biblical account will clear these questions up and give the proper answer, whether one is willing to accept it or not. We see in scripture that God made everything good and without the presence of evil. Yet, in doing so, God created man with moral freedom, and a will to choose between good and evil. God gave man a free will. That is the framework for the existence of evil. What does free moral choice really mean? Some argue that since God is good, why didn't He just create man undoubtedly good? He could have made us without the ability to choose. Yet, this would have defeated His reason for creating us in the first place. God made us with free moral choice so we could develop His attributes of character, and become like Him and have fellowship with Him. We were created for His pleasure. God's plan was to create something special. His long term purpose was to create additional members of His divine family. To achieve this, the development of divine character was essential to His plan. Hence, the need to create human beings as free moral agents. His choice then, was to create us with freedom. Without freedom we would never sin. Yet, without freedom we would never have the opportunity to choose our own future. We would not have love like God possesses. This is one of the most important of all the divine character traits of God. When God created man, He began the process of bringing forth children in His image **(Genesis 1:26).** We cannot force our own children to love us or do what's right. We can teach them these virtues and hope, as they grow, that they will choose to follow them in spite of the negative evil influences they may encounter. When God embarked on His plan to create children for Himself, who would have to choose to return His love, He also knew the risk! He was aware that they could choose an alternate way of life. He knew that there was choice that existed between good and evil. This is why there were rules of a standard set even in the Garden. What is a standard? "A standard is a pattern for guidance by which the excellence and correction of other things may be determined." We must remember man was not the first created entity to which God gave such a choice. When only God existed, there was no evil **(John 1:1)**. Long before the time of Adam, God created millions of spirit beings with the ability to choose. They are called *angels*. His intention was to produce beings who would accept His way and Love Him forever. Yet, of course, one of them made the wrong choice. How else could Lucifer decide to lift himself up if he didn't have the ability to choose to do so?

ORIGIN OF EVIL

Ezekiel 28 begins with God addressing the **"prince of Tyre,"** a human ruler of that ancient city along the Lebanese coast. Yet, starting in verse 11, the message shifts to the **"King of Tyre"** and it quickly becomes clear that no human being is meant here. The subject becomes the spiritual power behind the throne, the primary influence on the earthly ruler! This power is called a cherub, an angelic being **(verse 14)**. God says, you were perfect in your ways from the day you were created, till iniquity was found in you" **(verse 15)**. This angel was part of God's perfect creation. Yet, because he had freedom to choose, he had the capacity to choose evil. We read that "iniquity" or "lawlessness," was at some point found in him. His sin was the sin of pride. This was the first recorded instance of evil. **Isaiah 14** includes a similar description when God addresses the **"king of Babylon."** Yet, again the message switches to the spiritual power behind the throne. Starting in verse 12, Heylel (**Lucifer in Latin**) which means "Light Bringer," was a vessel of the light of God's truth. Yet, verse 13 shows he began to imagine evil in his heart. While we are not sure how long it took for this being to develop the way of evil in his heart, we do know it was all about self. Satan was the first **"moral relativist."** He denied absolute good and evil as defined by God and chose to define good and evil for himself. He decided to make his own rules. Sound familiar? So God changed his name to **"Satan,"** meaning "adversary." God created this angelic being as the "seed of perfection, full of wisdom, and perfect in beauty" **(Ezekiel 28:12)**, but he developed pride in his beauty

(verse 17). He corrupted his wisdom by getting caught up in his own self-importance. This was his choice. So, he turned himself into Satan. **Verse 16** says that he became filled with violence within. He ascended into Heaven to exalt his throne **(Isaiah 14:13). Revelation 12:23** speaks of this fallen angel as a dragon who influences a third of the stars (angels) **(Revelation 1:20)** with him. Satan induced one third of the created angelic beings to turn against God. The third of the angels who followed Satan chose to oppose God and to promote themselves above others. **In doing so, they became demons, "evil spirits." God did not put the evil in their minds, neither did He introduce evil to Lucifer. Lucifer was free to follow God's way or consider the alternative. God never forced Satan to go his way. He permitted him to ponder and finally choose the way of evil.** God drove Satan out of heaven. He fell to the earth like lightning **(Luke 10:18)**. The next we see of Satan is his appearance to Eve in the Garden of Eden as the serpent. Why was man exposed to evil? As I have already mentioned, God was creating His own children mortal human beings. They had to have free moral choice. So, the issue of evil once again had to be faced. The sooner the better, so God created two special trees in the Garden of Eden. The tree of life and the tree of the knowledge of good and evil. The tree of life represented an acceptance of God's way. The other tree represented a rejection of God's instruction and deciding between good and evil for oneself. It did not take long for the devil to present his alternate lifestyle of evil to Eve. The devil approached Eve by suggesting that God was not telling her the whole story and that both she and her husband could do better for themselves by adopting the other way of life. Adam and Eve made the fatal choice to follow Satan, so Satan became the ruler of this world **(John 12:21)** and the god of this age **(2 Corinthians 4:4)**. Thus God allowed our first parents to disobey Him. Yet, He would use this incident to help fulfill His plan to bring human beings into His divine family. The choice Adam and Eve made is why we still see so much suffering, violence, and killing in our world. Man is living in rebellion to God's plan. Thus, Cain rose up and killed his brother Abel, setting a course that mankind would follow from that point forward. Our civilization has been wracked by war because someone wanted something or wanted to be someone greater than he was.

WHY WOULD GOD ALLOW THIS?

God's intent was for His children to choose His way of love forever and never consider turning against Him. There has been an evil plan set in motion by Satan. In this present day, when people choose Wrong, they will experience consequences. The ultimate consequence is spiritual death or separation from God if we are not born again. Ultimately, God will not continue to permit evil to persist in a universe He rules (Romans 6:23). In the Book of Revelation, we see the final undoing of Satan and his cohorts. Then war, or killing, or suffering will not be taught or tolerated and the Creator will guide all men, women and children into His way of life without Satan influencing them to reject! **So, get it right! Stop blaming God for all the trouble in this world.** We are still living in a world of rebellious people that would rather be influenced by Satan than God! That's what this war is all about!

IDENTIFY HIM!

There are two battle fronts for every Christian warrior. They are the self-inflicted and the Satanic-inflicted. Look first at the self-inflicted. These are problems brought on by our own negligence, indifference or disobedience! Such as not paying our bills, taking care of our health, or not doing proper maintenance on our homes or auto. Or maybe not being a good employee at our jobs. Many professing Christians are not practicing good Christian behavior and when questioned, they try to blame all the wrongs in their lives on Satan. While it is true that Satan will certainly use anything possible to defeat us, it is also true that through our negligence or indifference, we create a lot of battles that we shouldn't have to fight. If this is not corrected, it will destroy our effectiveness for the kingdom of God and Satan will certainly be glad to take the credit for that. We need the spirit of discernment to fight properly. This gift will help us to understand whether the battle we are engaged in is one of our own making or if it is a Satanic attack. Again, if you don't really understand what is causing the problem, then you don't know who to fight.

SATANIC PROBLEMS

The devil will use anything or anyone he can to wage spiritual war against us. He will use people, such as family, friends, neighbors, coworkers and even strangers. He will use the job, the home, and the mechanical devices of our day, books, music, and the media! Anything! That's not to say that all these outlets are automatically wrong. Some of them can be used properly to advance our walk with God. Eventhough Satan uses people and things, our real enemy is not people or things. Our real enemy is the spirits that influence us or them. Paul uses four descriptive words to make us understand exactly what and who we are fighting with. We also see here four levels of warfare. **Ephesians 6:12 says, "For we wrestle not against flesh and blood, but against principalities, against powers, against rules of darkness of this world, against spiritual wickedness in high places."**

LEVEL 1: Principalities - meaning chief rulers or beings of the highest rank and order in the Satanic kingdom. Every single nation in the world has a principality over it.

LEVEL 2: Against powers - meaning those who derive power from and who execute the will of the chief rulers (principalities), such as supernatural influences in governments.

LEVEL 3: Rulers of Darkness – meaning the spirit world rulers, or Lords of the age, such as lust, depression, fear, perversions, anger, and spirits of pride.

LEVEL 4: Spiritual Wickedness – meaning spirits sent by Satan. In Ephesians 2:2, Satan is referred to as the "prince and power of the air." The enemy cannot set up a kingdom over an area unless man has first mapped it out and given it a name. Examples: Prince of Persia in **Daniel 10:13**, the Prince of Grecia in **Daniel 10:20**, and Paul's beast at Ephesus in **I Corinthians 15:32.**

In Revelation 2:12-13, we read about **"Satan's seat,"** where Satan dwelleth. This reveals to us that satanic influence and control ONLY resides where men have given THEIR will and authority to exercise. Satan did not do away with the angelic order of authority,

but kept it and uses it where men give him control. In this manner, he has gained some measure of control of many world systems and governments. We must remember, however, the enemy's domain is only territorial. HE IS NOT THE RULER AND CONTROLLER OF THE WORLD!

Psalms 24:1 says, "The earth is the Lord's; and the fullness thereof." We must know these things and then go forward expecting to release the captives of this generation through the power of the New Birth message. We need to put Satan and all of his cohorts on our most wanted list! We need to begin to charge instead of retreat.

PRAYER:

God give me the wisdom of the Word, also the gift of discernment so I may know and understand this foe that is coming against the children of light. Let me know everyday as I go forward you have given me the tools to win. In the Name of Jesus, I will win! Amen.

OUR SECRET WEAPONS

"No weapon that is formed against thee shall prosper; and every tongue that shall rise up against thee in judgment thou shall condemn...." **Isaiah 54:17**

There will always be a battle after every breakthrough in our walk and growth in God. That battle will focus upon one front. The Word of God in our lives.

THE WEAPON OF THE WORD

Where is your Bible? Is it laying on the dash of your car? Is it just lying on a table somewhere in your house? Or do you just leave it on your favorite pew at church for convenience?

While it is honorable to own a Bible and everyone should, I must remind you that merely owning one will not guarantee your victory over your enemy. We must open the Bible and get the Word in our mind and spirit, so like a seed, it can be planted in our spirit and it will begin to grow. The most used terms in scripture is "The Word of God," "The Word of the Lord," "The Lord said," and "The Lord spoke." This Word has a "life force" that is released in us when we read it, study it and meditate upon it. There is no other Book to date like the Bible. It is God in ink. It is God's thoughts, God's feelings about us and about life and eternity.

Yet, it's like any other book if you just own one and never read it! In fact, you may have a Bible or any other book for that matter and say you own it, it's yours. The truth, however, is you don't really own it until you read it and allow it to become a part of your life, your decisions, and your thinking process. We must use the awesome power of the Word to do war against the enemy.

I Peter 1:23 says, "being born again, not of corruptible seed, but of incorruptible, by the word of God, which liveth and abideth for ever."

Did you catch that?

The word lives and abides in us. Jesus said, "he that abideth in me and I in him shall bring forth much fruit." Our fruit is maturity and victory over our own flesh.

We must allow the Word of God to become a controlling factor in our lives. That is, our decisions and our responses to the things needed to be influenced by the Word of God at work in our lives. If we are going to be effective in this war, then we must stand and believe the Word of God even during times of testing. There will be many times of testing. In Numbers 21:8, we see the Lord instructing Moses to raise a brass serpent up in the midst of the people so that they would be healed from the bites of the fiery serpents.

The key word in the verse is looketh. It means to be occupied and influenced with what we are looking at. This is the equivalent of Abraham's refusing to consider his own body and waxing strong in faith by looking unto the promises of God. Does this mean that Abraham was ignoring his physical condition and simply saying I am not actually getting older? No, certainly not, There is floating around in the Christian community a so called faith that I call "voodoo" faith. That is those who embrace this mindset simply say, "Ignore the real situation, and don't acknowledge them in any way and they will just go away!"

Real faith, however, acknowledges reality, yet does not limit the outcome to the reality of the situation but allows a higher principal to begin to intervene. It's called faith in God's word.

Daniel never denied he was in a lion's den. The Hebrew brethren never denied they were put into a furnace. So what, then is the proper understanding of the above scripture about Abraham not considering his body and waxing strong in faith? Simply that Abraham did not merely allow his physical limits or the limits of the laws of nature to be the final determining factor. He didn't deny those things, he, simply acknowledged them, and looked to the power of God's promise in His Word that had been made to him!

The released Word produced life force in him as it does in us! We must use the Word properly in our lives for it to produce the proper results! Satan is always afraid of God's word when it is released properly into our lives and most certainly when it is used properly against him. He must come under subjection to God's word as must everything else. Jesus shows us how to use the Word in the wilderness temptation.

Notice when Jesus was faced with the temptation (**Matthew 4:11**), how Satan tried to tempt his flesh, his emotions, and his carnal reason. Jesus relied not on carnal reason or emotion to fight back, He released the power of the Word. Jesus knew the authority of the Word. Do we? In order for Satan to convince Adam and Eve to sin, he had to plant doubt in their minds about the Word of God. We all know the results of that. So, get the Word in your spirit.

What gives the Word of God authority? Because, it's God's word. The Word is God's check to us. You can have a box full of checks, yet if no name is attached to the checks and if the account isn't in good standing, the checks are useless. God's promises are checks that can be cashed by heavens' bank. It has His name on them. The world was formed and framed by the Word of God. That's real creative power. God wants to release that same power into our lives through His Word. What a weapon God's word is! So use it!! Don't go out without it!!

"Words are containers for power!"

WEAPON OF FAITH

Faith isn't a jump in the dark; it's a walk in the light. Faith is not guessing; it is knowing. We are made to operate in faith after God's design. We may not be able to see what God is bringing forth in our lives, but He wants us to believe it is there.

In a day when people are putting their faith in all kinds of things and all kinds of gods, we must know that real faith must be directed to God and His Word. For someone to merely say, "as long as I have faith in something, it will be alright," is not good enough! Faith in God is what God is going to honor. The fruit that is in our lives is the evidence of what and who we are in contact with. Therefore, it is imperative that we remain in touch with the source of power. We must know and obey God's Word. **In Mark 11:22-23,** we are told that we must have faith in God. Jesus is saying here that we need to have the God kind of faith! Some people put their faith in the faith of other people, yet we are instructed to put our faith in God!

We must use our weapon of faith. God's Word is very clear in the fact that God has given to everyone a measure of faith. God honors faith! **In Luke 18:8, Jesus asked the question "when the Son of Man cometh shall He find faith on the earth?"** In the climate of our world, were our faith is challenged daily, we must have a persevering faith to win this war. Persevering faith will drive back the enemy time and time again. Persevering faith will believe

God is at work even when you are experiencing nothing but delay. God is looking for this kind of faith today. There are times in our lives when we seek deliverance and miracles. Yet God wants us to just have persevering faith in Him to hold on. Our faith is what will move God to help us. Our faith is also what will drive the enemy out of our lives. Not our mood swings; not our emotional outbursts; not our threats but our faith that is settled in God.

Everyone understands that for a seed to produce, it must be planted in the soil. Of course, once it's in the soil you must leave it there. You can't try to dig it up every few days to see how it's doing. So it is with our faith. We must place our faith in God and His Word. We are made complete in Him **(Colossians 1:15-16).** As we obey God's Word, His power is released in us! This is why the Word of God is so powerful. So use faith as a weapon; become rooted in God and His Word. He is our strength because He is in us and us in Him. God is our true source of faith.

Don't let Satan talk you out of your faith! Many people say, "I have lost faith." This is a deception proposed by Satan. You can't lose faith; faith is God's gift to us. God has given everyone a measure of faith! So what do I mean? We may become discouraged and not use our faith. We may choose not to believe anything, yet, the fact is, faith is still in us. We are just not releasing it! Many use this terminology when they have given in to the enemy, simply given up or become weary in the battle. You don't loose your faith; you make a decision not to use it. Of course, the results are the same. The reason Satan wants people to believe they have lost their faith is so the spirit of hopelessness and despair can come upon the person.

So take God's gift and go to war against the Father of all liars. He wants to deceive you and your family to destroy all that God has for you. If you choose to surrender or not use your faith, then this could happen! The scripture tells us to whom so ever we yield ourselves, to him we become the servant thereof! God has created us to serve Him not sin and Satan.

Take the word of faith and drive Satan out of your world! God said we could and He said He will help us to do it! Scriptures on faith:

GENESIS 18:14; MATTHEW 8:13
NUMBERS 14:8; MATTHEW 9:22
DEUTERONOMY 31:8; MATTHEW 9:29
I SAMUEL 17:37; MATTHEW 17:20
I SAMUEL 17:46; ROMANS 10:17
I CHRONICLES 28:9; EPHESIANS 6:16
JAMES 1:6; HEBREWS 11:6
2 CORINTHIANS 6:10; HEBREWS 10:23

THE WEAPON OF PRAYER

When we pray, we open a door in the spiritual realm. In fact, we set in motion all kinds of things. Prayer begins to release and bind things. Through prayer, we discern what to release and what to bind. Satan cannot operate freely where prayer is being engaged. While prayer goes against the grain of our flesh, if we are to be victorious we will have to pray. We see from scriptures that when men and women engaged in prayer, great things happened and miracles transpired.

Our blessings and power are released to us through the avenue of prayer. Elijah prayed and God shut up the heavens. Paul and Silas sang and prayed and God shook the Philippian jail. Look at Moses. No mission was more majestic in purpose and results than that of Moses. None was more responsible, diligent or difficult. His mission teaches us the power of prayer. In fact, Moses himself, and what he did were the answer to prayer **(I Samuel 12:8).**

In fact, four times, even Pharaoh solicited the prayers of Moses for relief from the blows of God's wrath. Prayer deals directly with God. The prophet Jeremiah is told by the Lord to **"call unto me and I will answer thee" (Jeremiah 33:3).**

Do you need an answer today? Do you need God to shake something for you? Then you must pray.

God said to Ephraim, **"curse you, you came out to battle, you had the war face, the training, yet when it came time for the battle you ran!"** When we don't pray, we are running! Satan will do anything in his power to prevent us from engaging in prayer. Prayer drives Satan back. Prayer brings the power of God to us!

In I Thessalonians 5:17, we are instructed to pray always. It means to remain in an attitude of communion with God.

You must know that Satan will try to send enemies in our lives that will take our prayer time from us. Some of these hindrances may even be good things. Some people go to church weekly yet they never pray. Some sing in the choir, teach classes, and yet, never take time to pray. This will leave you weak regardless of how busy you may be. In fact, if you are so busy you aren't praying, then you are too busy!

Jesus drew His disciples away to a lonely place to pray, away from the noise, the hustle, and the busyness of daily life. We still need that today my friend. Some equate "spirituality" with how many times they are down at the church during the week. Yet busyness is no substitute for not praying. We are in a spiritual war!

Jesus did not just say if you can get busy enough you will be victorious. No, He said that it is through prayer that direction and strength come to us! Prayer is hard work. People that are spiritually lazy people and do not want to change will not pray. Neither will they be victorious! Satan is hoping that we of the house hold of faith will get so busy, even doing good things that we don't take time to pray. God has given us the weapon of prayer, yet, he will not force us to use it! Everything we do needs to be baptized in prayer. Through prayer we can see ourselves as God sees us. We can also see Satan for the deceiving, lying, defeated foe that he is! When you pray, Satan always leaves. Satan is no match for spirit filled praying!

You will not talk Satan into leaving you or your family alone. You can't sing enough to him to make him go away. You can't do enough "good things" that he will get discouraged and leave. Yet, when you begin to pray and release things in the majestic name of Jesus, then soon Satan's influences will leave and angelic influences will take its place. So Pray! Fight the fight daily and pray. Pray when you understand. Pray when you don't understand. Pray as Paul said, ALWAYS! Through prayer, lives are spared, and through prayer cities are released from the death hold of sin! Through prayer dead churches can be resurrected. Through prayer you and I can make war! So pray and give Satan a bad day instead of letting him give you a bad day!

James 5:16 declares, "The effectual fervent prayer of a righteous man availeth much."

THE WEAPON OF WORSHIP

Someone has said that our worship is "giving God goose bumps." The statement presupposes that God not only seeks our worship, but thoroughly enjoys it. I remind you that Satan's desire was to be like God and to be worshipped! Our worship is the summation of adoration, the expression of our highest congratulations. Worship is a magnification of God and minimization of self! Worship isn't for us; it's for God. Is it no wonder that Satan desires that we worship everything except God?

While it is true that God has no need of anything because of His nature, it is also true that God has desires. His top desire is to receive praise and worship from you and me. Our worship declares God's worthiness. **Psalms 48:1 says, "Great is the Lord, who is worthy of praise."** The Bible teaches us that we were "created for His praise." Worship honors God's holiness. In **Isaiah 57:15 God's holiness is called "high and lofty and holy."** Worship is always the proper response to our salvation. "I am He who blots out your transgressions for my own sake and remembers your sins no more (**Isaiah 43:25**). The phrase "for my own sake" declares that our salvation is for His glory. Satan cannot stay where God is being worshipped!

Worship moves God to manifest Himself to us. David declared that no matter where he went, God was already there. *If I ascend into the heavens thou art there or if I make my bed in hell thou are there!* God's spirit is everywhere in this universe. However, we must know that there is a difference in His presence merely being everywhere and His spirit being manifested! God's spirit is over every wicked city on the planet. It is apparent in some cases that the spirit of Satan is being manifested instead of the spirit of God because men have given themselves to sin instead of holiness! The worship of God will bring a manifestation of God. God manifested Himself in the garden. He came down and fellowshipped with Adam. The hot burning desert floor that Moses was so accustomed to turned into a holy place when there was a manifestation of God in a bush! Mt. Sinai, says the scripture, was "a smoke", it trembled and shook when God manifested himself there. The lion's den that Daniel was confined to became a "safe place" instead of a "death place" when there was a manifestation of God's power. Our worship will cause God to manifest Himself. When God shows up, Satan cuts out! **In 2 Chronicles 5:13-14, it says, "His glory filled the temple," this manifestation was referred to as the "Shekinah" glory of God.**

In the New Testament, God manifested Himself in the person of Jesus Christ and we are still feeling the effects of it. At Pentecost, He manifested Himself as the promise and the infilling of the Holy Spirit was the results thereof. Worship releases God's power, His intervention, and His deliverance. The presence of worship means the absence of despair, the absence of dejection, shame and discouragement. The prophet Isaiah challenges us to "give God our spirit of heaviness for the garments of praise" **(Isaiah 61:3).** Who gives us all these feelings of despair and hopelessness and heaviness? Our enemy, Satan. **Yet, God says have a worship service and I will come!**

Use your worship to drive out Satan and to bring in God. **Psalms 68:1 boldly proclaims, "Let God arise, let His enemies be scattered."** God did not create us to give our worship to Satan. He created us to worship Him. Drive out the spirit of heaviness in your life and in you home and have a manifestation of God. Worship Him and give Him "goose bumps!"

> **Psalms 34:1 says, "I will bless the Lord at all times, His praise shall continually be in my mouth."**

THE NAME OF JESUS A POWERFUL WEAPON

In this conflict we are engaged, we must take advantage of all that God has made available for us. The Name of Jesus is one such weapon. Satan and all his host cannot resist or overpower the Name of Jesus. We must use it! He has given us His name to use. I might add, not only to use, but to honor and to uplift. We are known in the spiritual realm by His name. We cannot only use it against the enemy. We can use it to bring blessings to others. We can use it to help ourselves.

John 14:14 says, "**If ye shall ask anything in my name, I will do it.**" That's a promise. **Yet, many try to use the name of Jesus as some "magic word" to be added on to the end of a prayer to get what they want. This, of course is not what the above scripture is implying. How then do we use the name of Jesus effectively?**

First of all, we must realize that we must, through obedience take on the name of Jesus in our relationship with God. We come in covenant agreement when we take on His name. We identify with the body of Christ. We set a level of authority in the spirit realm through the Name of Jesus. We begin to mature in our relationship with God when we pray in the spirit. Through the name of Jesus we are not merely praying for our selfish will to be done, we are through the spirit praying for the will of God to be revealed and then released. Many immature people try to take the promises of authority and power in the name of Jesus to use it to fulfill their selfish desires. Satan loves it when people do this. Of course, God doesn't honor this kind of "short cutting" and when it doesn't work Satan is always close by to give the immature person a double dose of unbelief and confusion. **I John 5:14-15** gives some insight about the proper use and the proper mindset we should have. **"And this is the confidence (the assurance, the privilege of boldness) which we have in Him. (We are sure) that if we ask anything (make any request) according to His will (in agreement with His own plan), He listens to us and hears us."** Verse 15 **"And in (service) we (positively) know that He listens to us in whatever we ask, we also know (with settled and absolute knowledge) that we have (granted us as our present possessions) the request made of Him."**

The power of the Name of Jesus can only be released when we are in covenant agreement with what He has commanded for us.

This is why it is imperative for us to obey God's word. The things that Gods words requires of us are not mere suggestions, they are commandments that when obeyed will without doubt bring great anointing, power, and maturity to our Christian life.

The Name of Jesus cannot be over emphasized. In Matthew 28:18, Jesus told His disciples "all authority has been given unto me in heaven and on earth." We must know it is God's will for us to be victorious and to know His will for the world, and for our lives. Once we understand this truth, and then when we speak His name, we will see results!

Trying to defeat Satan and be victorious without the proper understanding and use of the Name of Jesus is like trying to run a freight train without a track!

Anyone knows that even as powerful as a train's engine is, it cannot pull the load attached to it and reach its proper destination unless there is a track for it to travel on! It was made to travel on a track. It has to have a track.

So it is with us. The Name of Jesus is the track we must travel on. The infilling of the Holy Spirit is the fuel that runs our lives. Even if we have fuel and are not on the track, we still won't go very far! So get on track, and as Paul said, **"put on Jesus Christ and identify with Him."** Jesus is the family name of the Heavenly kingdom. Take it upon you. Use it to know the will of God. Release it to set people free. Declare it to drive the powers of the underworld back to the dark pit where they belong!

> **Philippians 2:8-9 says, "That at the Name of Jesus every knee should bow, in heaven, and on earth and under the earth."**
>
> **Scriptures that reveal the authority of the Name of Jesus:**
>
> **Isaiah 9:6; I Corinthians 1:24**
> **John 14:6; Romans 10:4**
> **Hebrews 1:3; John 11:25**
> **Colossians 2:10; Acts 4:12**
> **I John 1:1; Revelation 19:16**
> **Hebrews 13:8; Acts 2:38-39**

PRAYER:

In the Name of Jesus I ask that you give me greater understanding of the revelation of your name. That I may use the weapons of warfare wisely, thus securing not only my victory but the victory for those that I reach out to help as well. I repent of any disobedience that may be in my life. Let your spirit empower me daily to do your will. In Jesus' Name. Amen.

TAKING BACK LOST GROUND

"Shout, for the Lord hath given you the city." **Joshua 6:16**

Let's talk about reclaiming lost ground. We must now look beyond our selves. We must realize not only does God want us to be victorious, but He desires that we help others become victorious as well. I remind you that part of the mandate given the church was to go and make disciples.

A quick glance at the following statement will remind us of the confused and yet desperate state of many in our society.

Welcome to the Psychiatric Hotline

A. If you are obsessive-compulsive: Press 1 repeatedly.
B. If you are codependent Please ask someone to press 2 for you.
C. If you have multiple personalities: Please press 3, 4, 5, & 6
D. If you are paranoid-delusional: We know who you are and what you want. Just stay on the line so we can trace the call.
E. If you are schizophrenic: Listen carefully, a voice will tell you which number to press.
F. If you are manic-depressive: It doesn't matter which number you press, no one will answer.

While the above mentioned problems are very real for many, we are certainly in no way making light of real needs. We are only trying to drive the point home that our world is in trouble, Something must be done. God wants people to be well. God wants people to live in harmony and to enjoy the journey of life. It is time for the household of faith to go forward and reclaim our families, our cities, our nation, and our world for God. But how, you may ask?

First of all, by conducting spiritual warfare against the enemy of the souls of men. Secondly, by understanding the people we are trying to help! We must know how to minister to those in crisis. This is exactly what Jesus did in **Mark 5:1-20.** The definition of the word *crisis* (Greek - basanizo) is *to be harassed or distressed*. The term comes from the word *touch-tone* which means *to reveal the truth of the heart under pressure.*

A crisis is anything that breaks the normal pattern of life. It may lead to either growth or disaster. Also, it will often bring about a major turning point for either good or bad. You can't control the crises that come into your life, but you can control your reactions to those crises. Dealing with a crisis will often force us to grow spiritually and emotionally in an area that we would never choose for ourselves.

The major impact of a crisis is that it disrupts the normal balance in our lives. We live in a world where we juggle spiritual, emotional, and physical responses to life's challenges every day. People in crisis often lose control of their lives. They become out of touch with their own feelings and react in a variety of ways that they might ordinarily never choose under normal circumstances. These responses may include: A) Shock – some go into a state of psychological shock. B) Anxiety - a state of perpetual anxiety including nightmares, fears and phobias. C) Depression - falling into total hopelessness. D) Violence - such as suppressed anger and fear. E) False adaptation - that is "wishful thinking" and not dealing with reality!

This is the state of many today in the world and even some in the church. We must restore these people to their rightful place in God's kingdom. He wants us to have abundant life.

WHAT CAN WE DO?

If you read the story in Mark 5 where Jesus delivered a man in crisis, he was possessed of evil spirits. He really had a crisis, yet in this story, we see the Biblical approach to taking back lost ground. The very first truth that is apparent is this, that there is no place where Jesus won't go! He came to the region of the Gadarenses. To win the souls of Men, we must move out of our comfort zones where we spend a lot of time just ministering to each other. Not that we don't need ministering to! The truth is this, an army is amassed and trained to go into battle and not only to maintain a position, but to take control of more ground as well and then possess that land.

The same gospel that has delivered us will also deliver others. We are not called just to hold a position. We are called to go forth and conquer new ground as well. This story also shows us that there is no person Jesus can't save if they want help. Verse 2 gives the condition of this man's spirit when it states that he had an "evil spirit." We need to stop being content with just a little spot in our city, just a little victory every now and then, a little joy, and a little blessing. We need to declare war on the enemy and go forth and begin to minister to those in crisis in the power of the Holy Ghost. If we are not careful, we will have the mindset of those of the city in Mark 5. It says of them they could do nothing for this man so they separated themselves from him. They adjusted to the fact that he would just remain the way he was. They surrendered to the enemy! We must not think like this, we must know that all people can be touched by the power of the Name of Jesus. In fact, the greatest harvest is now! So don't give up on those in your work place, in your home, and in your city. Fight for this freedom. This story also teaches us there is no problem that Jesus can't solve. In verse 8 of Mark 5, we read the Master saying, **"come out of Him"** speaking to the unclean spirit. Of course, this man was delivered.

God wants to deliver people. He wants to deliver entire cities!

Then in verse 19 and 20, we see this man delivered and in his right mind and clothed. Jesus' command to Him is **"go home and tell them what I have done for you."** Jesus had taken back what the unclean spirits had taken from the man's life. Like many in that city, many today seem to be more comfortable with people living in crisis than with those who have been delivered! We must break this mindset. Satan has come to steal, to bind, and to destroy. Yet, we have been called to war against the powers of darkness and take back the souls of men imprisoned by sin and desperation. If the army of God's kingdom doesn't do this, there is no one else to do it! **Luke 10:19 says, "Behold, I give unto you power to tread on serpents and scorpions, and over all the power of the enemy; nothing shall by any means hurt you."** Man has only one adversary in this world. It is not sickness. It is not slavery. It is not war, or crime, or poverty or death. These are just the by-products of the power that lurks behind all cruelty. It is the driving force behind all evil. It is the devil.

Yet, when we go forth in the power of our King, and make war, the devil will submit and the devil will obey the command of God's authority and he will cease his oppressions. **Luke 10:17 declares,**

"And the seventy returned again with joy, saying, Lord, even the devils are subject unto us through thy name."

God gives the invitation in **I Peter 5:7** to **"cast all your cares on God for He careth for you."**

I think it's time we gave the devil permission to do one thing only, and that is to stare at the bottom of our feet while we walk over him. Are you tired of your family being bound? Are you weary of being the tail and not the head? Then, declare war on the enemy. God has never amended His Word. He did not say "some of my followers will cast out devils, for a little while, and then the power will disappear." The word still says **"in my name you shall cast out devils."**

A DESENSITIZED WORLD

The devil is a deceiver. He knows that an alert, vigilant believer will recognize his attacks. So he tries to bring us to a place of complacency where we will not recognize his works. He wants to desensitize our cities, our lives, our hearts and our minds to the point where sin no longer even troubles us.

Our society has become desensitized to the point where we see murder and it doesn't even slow us down any. Our world has seen so much of it on television and in movies that it has very little impact on us any longer. We don't even blink when people openly talk about gross sexual sins. We listen to profanity pouring out of the television, out of the radio, and out of the CD players. Gutter talk abounds! We have become comfortable with what the world offers.

Here is a greater tragedy. We have become desensitized in the spirit realm. There are intruders in the garden and we do not even know they are there. Many churches are desensitized. They meet weekly in their "holy huddles" to talk about how great they are and how bad the world is. Yet, it never dawns on them that we have been given the power to set the world free. We must break through this mindset. Our churches are training centers and field hospitals to help people recover, not shrines to be worshipped. Too many have already been lost in this battle. We must turn the tide and go forward to take back lost ground.

GUARD THE TERRITORY

Once victory has come, we must then guard our territory. Whether it's our life or the entire body of Christ, we must stop allowing the atmosphere of our homes and lives to be conducive for the manifestations of hell. Notify every devil that you know that they are defeated. Announce to every spirit trying to gain entry that the great God lives in you. Give no place to the devil.

Behind every situation we face there are spiritual powers and rulers of darkness at work. We must not only overcome but we must destroy every stronghold the enemy has built in our homes, our cities, and our nation. We must guard the territory we have reclaimed. We do this by prayer, by getting the word in our spirit and by being in the body of Christ.

Jesus said "If ye abide in me, and my words abide in you, ye shall ask what ye will, and it shall be done unto you" (John 15:7).

God is looking for people that are willing to commit. He is looking for workers, worshippers, and warriors. If we are ready, so is God!

PRAYER:

God give me spiritual insight to know how to witness, pray and minister to those in my world. Let me guard my mind, my heart and my life that your light may shine through me. That others may see it and come to you. I release spiritual power, and strength into my life that I may go forth and regain what Satan has taken away. In Jesus' Name Amen.

BEHIND ENEMY LINES

"Ye shall chase your enemies and they shall fall before you by the sword." **Leviticus 26:7**

It is time for the special forces of God's great army to come to the forefront. In military terms, there are those who go into an area of conflict and begin to set the stage for an invasion. They are referred to as special opts. In most cases their pictures or their names are never published in the news media. Part of their training is to remind them this war is not about them there is a higher purpose. So it is with kingdom warfare. Those who will be in the special forces, who will go behind enemy lines, will be mature enough to understand it's not important that they get recognition, but that our Commander in Chief Jesus Christ gets all the recognition!

These special forces will be skilled in prayer and in the rightly dividing of the word. They will have a deeper understanding about releasing the spiritual authority of God! They will not be driven by impatience. Impatience is the fruit of pride! A proud person cannot seem to wait for anything with the proper attitude. They will walk by faith even under pressure. They will have confidence in the Word of God and not just in an emotional feeling.

Their mindset will not be to just stay in some comfort zone somewhere and be content. These warriors of the eternal God see the BIG Picture. They know the end is near. They understand the time for revival is now! They know that one plus God is a majority.

WHAT SATAN DOESN'T WANT YOU TO KNOW!

In Revelation 2:12-13, we read about "Satan's seat, where Satan dwelleth."

What does this tell us? This reveals to us that satanic influence and control ONLY resides where men have given him THEIR will and authority to exercise. Satan did not do away with the angelic order of authority, but kept it and uses it where men give him control. In this manner he has gained some measure of control of many world systems and governments. The enemy's domain is only territorial.

HE IS LIMITED

Satan has many limitations. He is not as powerful as many proclaim him to be. Something to consider. Why do people let Satan work in their lives? Many do not understand the truth about Satan's network of evil. Of course, Satan doesn't want us to know this either. He is not what many think he is. He is not equal with God.

Remember, he was cast out of heaven for declaring himself equal with God. It was the original sin in heaven. Lucifer dared to exalt himself to be like God. It is wrong for Christians to speak of Satan as being equal with God. You are never more like Satan than when you are trying to get the glory for something!

He is a fallen angel. He is subject to the limitations of an angel. He is counterpart to an angel, certainly not God.

He is not all powerful. Only God has all power. Satan's power is limited by what God allows him to do on earth. In **I John 4:4 we read, "ye are of God, little children, and have overcome them; because greater is he that is in you, than he that is in the world."** Satan's power is also limited in regard to us as to what we allow him to do. Though he does not have the "all knowing" power of God, he does have more knowledge than mere humanity. Satan has been studying humanity's habits for 6,000 years. He is more aware of the end time than many in the church are! He does listen intently to our conversations. So we need to speak the right things.

HE IS NOT OMNIPRESENT

God fills the universe. Because Satan is a fallen angel, he is limited to one place at a time. He can go from place to place as swiftly as an angel, but cannot be at two places at once. This is where satanic command comes into play. He orders spirits to go to and fro doing his bidding. He cannot read your mind or know your thoughts.

We can pray in our mind (silently) or in the spirit (in tongues), and he cannot know what we are asking God. You can also bind him from listening to your prayer.

He doesn't even know if the temptations he drops in your mind are working unless you manifest them outwardly or dwell on them.

When you are tempted, start thinking good thoughts, pray, think of worship songs, and give God praise. The evil thoughts will flee and Satan's strategy is defeated.

Unfortunately, the normal christian will not take the time to know their enemy, or for that matter, really understand the battle plan that God has made available that gives us total victory over our enemy.

In 2 Corinthians 2:11 it says, "Lest Satan should get an advantage of us: For we are not ignorant of his devices." Those who will go behind enemy lines to secure the souls of men and help liberate their cities will be those who are not ignorant of his devices.

One of Satan's greatest weapons is the weapon of deceit, and what we believe about him. The scripture refers to us understanding his strategies of operation! In military terms, if you know the next move of the enemy or where he is headed, then you can prevent it from happening. When we engage the weapon of prayer and fasting, it's like sending up a stealth bomber with radar. We can pinpoint the enemy's movement and respond accordingly. Where there is much prayer there is much power. Satan can't handle a warrior who prays and fasts.

In our modern day military forces they have what they call night vision goggles. These specially made goggles enable the warrior to see in the dark. The prophet declared that gross darkness would cover the earth in the latter day. The idea here is spiritual darkness with sin darkening the mind of reason, destroying the conscience as though it were injured beyond feelings. This, of course, is the condition of many in this present society.

Yet through prayer and releasing the Word of God into our lives we will be able to see through the darkness. Divine revelation is our night vision. This is why we must know who Jesus really is. We must have a clear understanding of His Word and how it can be applied to our current situations! Many are on the edge of fulfillment, yet because of the spiritual darkness, they can't see their victory coming! So put on your night vision equipment so you may see what is really going on! In fact, when we begin to see the battle from God's perspective, we will see the enemy running for cover. We will be able to expose him and ultimately drive him out.

In Hebrews 12:22 we read, "But ye are come into Mt. Zion and into the city of the living God, the heavenly Jerusalem, and to an innumerable company of angels."

Once you go behind enemy lines you have the assistance of the angelic host. God will send reinforcement to help us do battle. **In Revelation 20:1-3** we see an angel coming from heaven having a key to the bottomless pit and a great chain in his hand to bind Satan. This can only happen once the power of Satan has been broken. That's where the end time church comes in. God is calling us to move behind enemy lines and start shining light in all the dark places. Thus driving out our enemy.

Remember those who serve behind enemy lines don't really care who gets the credit as long as the territory is secured and the victory is gained. We are not self assured; we are God-assured. We must release the peace of God that Paul said will pass all human reasoning!

Our victory never comes from our emotions or our intellect. Our victory comes by refusing to judge by what our eyes see, what our ears hear, and by trusting that what God has promised will come to pass.

GET A PLAN OF ATTACK

No one goes into enemy territory without having a plan of attack and a step by step procedure to see that it is carried out. In this spiritual war we are coming into the enemy's territory or actually territory that men have given over to him. If men have given Satan control we can take back that control. We must go into the spiritual "death zones" and speak life.

VERBALIZE YOUR RESISTANCE TO SATAN

Resist the devil and he will flee from you (James 4:7).

What does this mean? It means to fight offensively, not just defensively. It means taking the initiative instead of sitting down somewhere and just waiting to see what might happen! We need to speak the Word of God to our situations. We need to verbally speak to the enemy. Let him know we are not going to lose this battle. We need to declare, "Satan take note and listen. You will not conquer me. I am blood-washed, spirit-filled, and daily delivered, strongly sanctified, spirit-soaked, and word-indwelt. I am linked with sovereign and eternal power through the mighty name of Jesus. I won't be deceived, detoured, derailed, distorted, distracted, discouraged, or disillusioned by your schemes. You parade yourself as an "angel of light", yet I walk in a greater light. My life is off-limits to you. My door is closed to you. You won't walk in, crash in, slither in, sneak in, pry in, jump in, dive in or barge into my life. I have authority over you in Jesus' Name. Your days are numbered, your kingdom doomed, your designs dwindling, your evil eroding, your deceit is decaying, your deception diminishing, and your death is dying. Your progress is poisoned, your poison is paralyzed. Your ultimate victory has been canceled, and soon your show will be over!

You can't trap me with your wares or soil me with your suggestions. I am an over comer by the word of my testimony. I have come to you in the name of the Lord to drive you out of my life, my church, my city, and my family!

Stop right now and speak these things then shout the victory!

STAY CLEAN!

When we go behind enemy lines to lead people that are bound into freedom, we also drive back the powers of darkness. Our efforts against Satan are weakened when we engage in ungodly living.

Many today live impure lives and don't understand why their lives go from bad to worse. We must remember God's bottom line desire for us is not that we just be happy, but that we be holy. Don't expect to win any battles while living an unholy life!

We must wear the Christian armor at all times. We must wear it in our marriages, our families, our businesses and our social lives. Only a life totally devoted to Jesus Christ and His Word will survive the raging battles to which we are all exposed. So, remember if you are going to be a warrior for God in these last conflicts, you must always be a warrior. God can't use weekend warrior!

This war will soon be over and then we shall hear our great commander say, "well done good and faithful servant." Until then, we must fight, take, and maintain new territory.

Our churches need to become centers of deliverance. Our churches need to become the spiritual seat of authority in our areas. There is no reason for our cities to stay in bondage! Put on your armor, blow the trumpet of victory, go forward, and we will be victorious. Remember the master has declared, **"He that endureth to the end, the same shall be saved."**

PRAYER:

God, I realize what a mighty church I am a part of and that we do not wrestle against flesh and blood, but with principalities, with powers, with world rules of the present darkness. Remind me that I am engaged in war, that I daily live on a battleground, not a playground. Grant me the courage to put on the whole armor of God so I may successfully pull down strongholds and perform great exploits in the power of your spirit. In Jesus' Name. Amen.

"Nor is there salvation in any other, for there is no other name under heaven given among men by which we must be saved." Acts 4:12

www.ingramcontent.com/pod-product-compliance
Ingram Content Group UK Ltd.
Pitfield, Milton Keynes, MK11 3LW, UK
UKHW041955230426
12048UKWH00008B/357